I Don't Like Pie and Mash or Jellied Eels!

Eleanor Beatrice Locke

Published by New Generation Publishing in 2018

First Edition

www.newgeneration-publishing.com

 New Generation Publishing

For Bob

One of the worst, albeit well meaning, pieces of advice that people give you after a bereavement is, 'You need to let go'. You may smile and nod, but you never take the advice because you can't. But I have come to realise that not letting go can become a positive energy, if you allow the sentiments to embrace you properly. This book emerged from feelings of despair which have now become happy memories.

This is me not letting go!

Contents

The Day it all changed for me

I haven't been back for thirty years or more. I expect changes but imagine same. I know it can never be, but I have hoped, anticipated perhaps there will be reminders of those growing up days. I have a thousand images in my mind of places and people. My life is changing so fast that I would find comfort in sameness and familiarity. Walking up the stairs at the station, I hope for the old wooden ticket office in the middle of the entrance hall, even though the walls are now brightly painted and the signs shiny and colourful. There had been a quaintness to the old peeling, faded, damp and dingy décor I remembered so well. The ticket office is now behind a window in the wall, and ticket machines and automated barriers adorn the foyer. The old hut is not there. It is now like all other underground stations. And the changes were to continue for me that day.

We are here to visit the university. My daughter is to study Chemistry at her chosen establishment and we are viewing and she is being interviewed.

This place is vast. What happened to the intricate mazes of Victorian terraces, once home to aunts, cousins and friends? Where are the grand houses with lofty iron railed steps leading to heavy black painted doors and brass knockers lovingly polished every day? These three and four storey houses were homes to extended families of several generations or housed more than one family. They have faded into memories. Gargoyles adorning the wall posts are just ghosts now, but once, the mythical creatures looked out at barefoot, ragged children playing Tin Tan Tommy and ball games like Pig in the Middle. They are now replaced by a sorry substitute; not their equal. These mansions of glory are swallowed up by the vastness of this 'Brave New World' they call campus. It consists of blocks of tiny compact, identical rooms, with everything needed for bright young minds to reach their academic goals.

There are custom build computer desks, abundant shelving, Wi-Fi infinity and standard single beds tucked neatly against the wall. Standing here whilst my daughter checks out the little shower room, I wonder where I am. Is this the spot where we played in Georgina Clark's basement home and ran long playing records at 78RPM instead of 33, rolling on the floor with laughter at 'Long Tall Sally' at triple speed and high voice? I remember Tollet Street, where we changed an l to i so that it said Toilet Street. Such was our unsophisticated childish humour.

Mid campus there stands a square of iron railings enclosing an area within. This is a relic from the past. The railings have spiked tops forbidding anyone who dares to breach them with impalement or death. On close examination we see that within its perimeter lies permanent residents. It is a graveyard. My daughter laughs and asks if this is part of the student accommodation. I reply in jest and say that it's where they put chemistry students who accidently blow up or gas the laboratory. This World War 1 graveyard, as it really is, cannot be disturbed and therefore remains as a reminder that we are mortal and children of destiny not always of our own choosing. Ironically, social housing for the living was expendable but housing such dead as these, non-negotiable. My daughter is unimpressed at the idea of coming to a university with its own graveyard. Perhaps this was one of the factors which prompted her to refuse the place she was offered here.

For myself I am in awe of the growth of this place. As a child, I could see some of the college buildings from my bedroom window. There was the grand white building with marble steps leading up to huge wooden carved doors. This building was named for the Queen. Then there was another hall for 'The People' and I could see two academic blocks. There was building work carried out on the latter, and the builders assembled a large round neon sign advertising their name, Harry Neal. I thought that the moon had fallen on the roof of the building and imagined all sorts of horrors. But my father told me that it wasn't the real moon, just Harry Neal's moon. I always called it so after this. The university was small then, no campus; just a few buildings. When I was ten years old, I ventured into the building with a classmate. We were doing a project on places in the locality and we two chose the college. A student showed us around the engineering department and gave us samples of metal shavings of various alloys. We felt very grown up and intelligent. At grammar school, we always had prize giving at the Peoples Palace Hall.

The university now occupies an extensive area which I knew as streets, shops and pubs and waste ground.

When we see as much as we want to see of the establishment, we wander across the road and through the flats to the place where I grew up. The two houses that had been our family homes, don't look much different. That is a comfort. However the alleyway running alongside is now blocked by huge padlocked iron gates. We used to ride our bikes, scooters and roller skates through the network of allies which joined the streets and squares. People used them as short cuts to the station. Playing in my garden I became familiar with those who used them regularly as a

3

throughway to the main road. I would wait for them. Kaye would come through in her blue school uniform and hat and later on her older sister Mimi would rush through after her working day, anticipating supper, ready on her return. Mr Lewis would come through shortly after and tip his hat at me as he passed. Nanny Smith would stop and admire my dolls and teddies as I roleplayed cooking their tea and scolding them for not behaving. I would never have played with the kids in the squares or the next street if gates had barred the way. How limiting life is nowadays. Fun and adventure sacrificed for safety and wellbeing of a kind!

We are to meet Peggy, one of my cousins who still lives in the area. She has an appointment at the doctor's surgery in 'The Old Road'. It isn't really called The Old Road and I don't know why we called it that but we always did. We make our way to the meeting point a pub near the university. This place is obviously popular being the only pub left for as far as you can see. At one time, standing outside here, you could see at least half a dozen others. What became of: The Globe, The King's Head, The Chimney Sweep (I used to call it that because the sign hanging outside, had a picture of a chimney sweep with all his brushes) and the Old Horn? I used to sit on the steps of the Chimney Sweep with Arthur, the landlords son and my classmate. His father would bring us out Tizer to drink, and crisps with the little screwed up packet of salt inside which you could never shake on because it was always damp! All these places are turned into fried chicken shops, mini supermarkets or new university buildings. This place was never a pub. It was the former home of the famous explorer, Captain Cook, and there was a small museum to his memory. Later it became a small local theatre. It is a listed building and has been taken over by a chain of public houses which often buy listed buildings but promise to preserve original features when transforming them into pubs.

After Peggy, we are to travel to the Midlands for another university interview next morning. I go with a heavy heart and fear that my life will suffer the worst and most inevitable change of all. I call the hospice before I leave and am told that stability prevails. Then a friend calls from the hospice and tells me that the nurses are saying that I should be there. And I know that I should, but he made it clear that our daughter's future is not to be compromised. So we travel. We are booked into a hotel where the two of us stayed many years ago, before the birth of our daughter. My husband was on a business trip and it was during the school holidays, (I was a teacher). The hotel was modern with bright décor and friendly staff. But that has changed too. It is quite run down and dismal. It is a miserable place to receive the awful news. The demise of the place which is nearing its end parallels the ending for the person with whom I had spent my first happy visit here.

My strong and brave daughter goes ahead with her interview and then we embark on our tearful return home. I know that life will be very different from now on.

My daughter did not choose either of these universities. The one she chose was also in the midlands. It is a beautiful place, set in glorious countryside. On first impressions, I had considered the university she chose as a little too modern and clinical, but I have come to love this place and I visit often. I spend many happy hours roaming the surrounding country and picturesque towns and cities.

She of course did not even consider the London College, with its built in graveyard, but I think about the day I went back. How many stories are lost in those streets and alleyways, flats and parks? Here are some of them.

University of Warwick

The Start of it all

I was born in the hospital which backed onto the university. My mother was forty years old when she discovered her unexpected pregnancy and from then on, was constantly worried that her baby would not be 'normal' because of her age. After I was born, came an intense dose of what they referred to as the baby blues. Then my sister Ann married and immigrated to Canada. This was the onset of depression. They didn't call it bipolar syndrome in those days and she was diagnosed with a mental illness and eventually recommended for admission to a psychiatric hospital.

I don't remember missing her, and I didn't really understand that she wasn't there or why, but I do remember that sometimes she was there. She came home at weekends, and so for a year of my very young life, I had a weekend mother.

My father of course continued working, and I was looked after by my Auntie Ethel and Uncle Jim. When Auntie Ethel began looking after my Grandfather, I was taken to the local council run day nursery. I hated it on the whole. I had never been an afternoon sleeper, and we were forced to go to bed for an hour after lunch. I persistently tried to get up and they always pushed me down again. I think that the nurses were quite kind really but I tested their patience. There were two things I liked there.

I loved playing with water in the troughs. I felt very calm as I ran my hand through the warm bubbly water pushing toy fish and boats. I even liked the smell of the rubber aprons we had to wear when playing with sand and water. The smell was exotic, as if it had no place in a building that smelt of leftover dinner and soiled nappies. The other thing I liked was when my father appeared at the door in his beige raincoat and brown hat. It meant that I could go home.

I liked it when my mother was home even though I

didn't have much concept of her being away. She would sit me up on the kitchen counter at night and wash me with a warm soapy flannel. Then on with my pyjamas, and I was ready for bed. I would even have a story. It was real luxury.

She was a pretty woman with light brown hair which she backcombed and smoothed over at the surface to create a beau font effect. She had deep hazel eyes which, even to a small child like me, spoke her moods. On the night when I came home from nursery and she was there, her eyes gleamed like sunlight on blue lakes. But on Sunday afternoons, they became sad and looked dull and muddy. Anticipating the parting after Sunday lunch, did not suit her eyes well. To me it had become a constant of my infanthood. These familiar happenings ended one day and my mother became an outpatient. I was then able to stop going to the nursery, and I never went to bed in the afternoon again. Even now, when I am unwell, I try not to stay in bed during the day.

When my mother did have hospital appointments, I was entrusted to the care of a woman called Maggie, who lived in the flats across the road. I was not sure what was worse, the nursery or Maggie's. I didn't mind Maggie herself. She was a tall slim woman with dark curly hair and freckles. She never wore powder or lipstick like mother, and she looked quite pale. It was Maggie's elderly mother who bothered me. She lived there. She was stern looking and had iron grey hair, and she always wore a floral pinafore as if she was about to pick up a feather duster and spring into action, and clean the room. But she never did. She sat in an armchair by the fire and that was Nanny Dyer's place. She had small round beady eyes which followed, watched and scrutinized my every move. She seemed particularly keen to watch what my hands were doing. Quite often Maggie who could be a little heavy handed, pulled my trousers up too high and I would be quite uncomfortable under the crotch and would try to tug under there to loosen them. Nanny would point her finger at me and tell me that I would get germs if I touched there because it was dirty.

The worst thing about Maggie's was when her children came home from school. There were two of them. Paula was a stout, red headed girl and John who was older, had dark wavy hair and was thin like Maggie. Paula used to call me Ellie Belly and teased me constantly and John just grunted at me as if I was an unwelcome stray cat getting in the way. They rarely played with me and if they did they always made sure that I got the worst deal, and they often used the game to ridicule me and laugh at me, just as Estella did to Pip, when she played cards with him and Miss Haversham looked on!

One day John built a tower with playing cards and as I walked past I caught it with my slipper and it tumbled down. John lost his temper and began shouting at me then punched me hard in the chest. Nanny Dyer said nothing but I wailed loudly which brought Maggie in from her kitchen chores. John was sent to his room until I was collected.

When my mother's appointments became occasional, I spent a lot more time at home and that was better, although she did lose patience with me sometimes.

I started school when I was five and my mother took a part time job in my father's firm. This suited her nerves better, to be physically and mentally occupied and to feel useful and slightly more independent.

When Sharon Could Run

Everybody knew everybody in our street. That was how it was. Doors were always open, usually the back doors, and all the women were called auntie and the men were called uncle. Most women stayed at home. They were full time housewives and mothers. The men handed over the weekly housekeeping money every Friday night, payday, and the women always complained that it wasn't enough because everything was getting more and more expensive. We all got our pocket money on Friday evening as well. I got a shiny silver sixpence and so did Sharon, but Kevin only a three penny bit. That's because he was younger. It was all I used to get when I was young, but now that I was five, I got more. Saturday morning was a mad rush to Arthur's, the local newsagents and sweet shop. Sharon often bought the Beano or Dandy but I hated comics, they were boring. I only bought them if there was a good free gift included, like the time the Dandy was giving away a boomerang that went bang when you threw it. I usually spent my money on sweets or an ice lolly. My favourite lolly was a Mount Everest. It was shaped like a pyramid and it was white and tasted of sweet, sweet lemons. Although it was ice, it was sort of a creamy texture that stayed on your tongue and melted slowly, then it gave a sour lemon after taste that made you shudder, it was delicious.

Some of the women had part time jobs. My mother did two days in a shop, but Sharon's mum Auntie Maureen, was a waitress. She worked most afternoons. The women were always prepared to look after each other's children for an hour or so; while shopping was done, or a visit to the hairdressers took place, or the doctors or dentist. Most of the time when we weren't at school, we played out. It was quite safe. There were two railed grass areas and pavements between the grass and the houses. We didn't need to go near the road and there was very little traffic anyway. We knew about not talking to strangers but we rarely saw strangers, except for the men and women who visited Auntie Vera and Uncle Jack, but that was another story.

There were quite a few of us who played out. Kevin was the youngest, he was only four, I was nearly six and Sharon was seven. Matthew was the big boy, he was ten. He didn't play out very much, and I was glad because he was horrible to me. I never knew why and I never asked, even when we were adults and Matthew was married, and we would laugh about when we were kids. I think he had probably forgotten by then, that he was horrible to me. We are all good at forgetting our more negative deeds.

We loved sitting on the pavement outside Mrs Rust's house and chalking on the floor. It was a good place to do it because not many people passed by that way and so our chalking didn't get rubbed out by lots of feet. Chalking was good because Sharon couldn't run. Another good pass time was playing mums and dads. Sharon didn't have to run for that either. She was always the mum and Kevin had to be the much bossed around dad. I was the kid. Matthew wouldn't play because it was too babyish and he was ten. Sharon was the eldest in the game and she was the boss. We both looked up to her particularly me, and she knew it. I did what she said, played what games she chose and she knew that she controlled me.

Whilst we played for hours and hours, all the aunts would congregate in one of the kitchens and drink tea. They talked about all sorts of things; often other neighbours. They talked about Vera in particular, but also about Pat at number thirty one who did not clean her toilet bowl properly, and about the distinct smell of fish that came from Albert's van when you walked past it. This was not surprising as his job was delivering fish from Billingsgate market to local chip shops. They never talked about the van in front of Auntie Sheila because Albert was her husband. I often heard them say, 'during the war we did this or that', as if it had been some bygone golden age which they remembered with great nostalgia and affection.

11

Then there was stuff we weren't supposed to hear, usually about Vera. One day some leaflets came through our doors' they were red in colour and there was a picture on the front of a stern looking man with glasses and wearing a military uniform. Unknown to the likes of children, it was a cold war, political propaganda tract of some kind, warning about a communist activist who could be a threat to world peace. As I walked in; the aunts were in my kitchen today; they were discussing what would happen if there was another war. I didn't really understand, but I had heard that people got bombed and killed in a war and it scared me half to death. I began crying very loudly because there was going to be a war. The aunts and my mother all began fussing• around me trying to assure me that there wasn't. Auntie Maureen said that God wouldn't let another war happen and neither would Mr Kennedy or Mr Khrushchev. I didn't know who these people were but thought that they must be friends of God who would help him stop a war. I was easily reassured by the thought that we were all safe and well in the hands of God, Kennedy and Khrushchev.

There was nothing more exciting to us children, than receiving new toys. We really valued them, and would brag unashamedly, showing them around. A new doll was like treasure, and my first two wheeler bike with stabilizers gave me pleasure beyond belief. Sharon went to Spain for her holiday that summer and she brought back a huge, shiny, multi-coloured beach ball. We could play catch or kick, as long as Sharon didn't have to run. Then one day my parents bought me a plastic toy record player which really played records. They had to be special records of which there were two free with the player. One was a bright pink vinyl disc and it played, 'Oh Susannah don't you cry for me', and the other was bright orange and played, 'Turkey in the straw'. I sat on the doorstep, proudly playing them and all the others gathered round mesmerized. I guess it was the equivalent of a new Xbox nowadays.

One day we were outside chalking. Mrs Rust had bought us some beautiful thick coloured chalks. She was a very kind woman and even though she was elderly and had white hair, she liked children and was always nice to us. Whilst we chalked on the pavement Matthew decided to grace us with his presence. He sat beside us and after a few minutes his face began to contort, and he burst out, "This is boring, why can't we play run outs or football on the grass?"

"Because Sharon can't run," I said.

Then his face became rigid and he snapped, "Who asked you stupid Ellen?" Then he grabbed a piece of chalk and began drawing furiously giving running commentary as he did so. "This is Ellen getting run over by my bike ha ha ha, and now Ellen gets hit in the face by the ball. Ellen's face gets all smashed up." Then he scribbled all over the face he had drawn.

Next he press ganged Kevin into playing football with him. He made a goal with two large stones and four year old Kevin was forced to be goalie against ten year old Matthew who came charging towards him, scoring then ran around in a circle like a demented dog yelling, "Goaaaal----!" and whooping loudly.

Sharon couldn't run, it was a fact and I just accepted it. I didn't fully understand why, but when I asked her she said that it was because of her heart. That didn't really help, and I was no wiser. I heard the aunts talking one day in Kevin's kitchen; it was one of the conversations I wasn't supposed to overhear; and they were saying that she was a 'blue baby'. So I imagined a bright blue baby and thought it must have really scared Auntie Maureen when she first saw her. They also said that Sharon had a hole in her heart. I wondered how she had got that, and why she wasn't bright blue anymore. One day my mother told me that Sharon was going away and that she might not be back. So I asked if she was going to Spain with Auntie Maureen and Uncle Mike again. But my mother said that she was going to hospital. Well my mum was always going to hospital, when I was three she went there every week and stayed all week. But on Friday she always came home, and I couldn't understand why Sharon might stay there for ever. So I asked if Auntie Maureen and Uncle Mike were moving to the hospital, like Jane from the money lender's square had moved to Wales, which was another country just like Spain was another country and not in England. My mother then began to change her story and say that Sharon probably was coming back and they weren't moving at all. It was all a bit strange.

I didn't see Sharon before she went. Two days later Auntie Maureen was in our kitchen having tea and looking very sad. My mum was telling her that she needed to keep busy and that it would make the time go quicker. During the following weeks I played with Kevin a lot, it was great fun finally getting to be the boss, because now I was the oldest. I got to be the mum and Kevin was the kid. This lasted for a few weeks.

Then one morning I woke up to the sound of something tapping rhythmically outside. I ran to the window and pulled back the curtain. Sharon was outside wearing a yellow dress and bouncing the big beach ball from Spain. Auntie Maureen and Uncle Mike were outside too and a little black dog was running around on the grass. I was so excited and I ran into my parent's room yelling, "I want to go out! Sharon is back and she's playing out." My mum said that it was only six o'clock and told me to go back to bed. Later on when I was allowed out, Sharon said that she couldn't play because the newspaper people were coming round. I didn't understand this because they delivered newspapers every day and it never stopped us playing.

Two days later though, my parents were very excited when the papers came, and they spread them out on the kitchen table for me and my sister Lizzy to look at. There on the front page of all three papers was Sharon in her dress; which you couldn't tell was yellow because pictures in the papers were all grey; and she was bouncing her ball from Spain. The dog, which turned out to be her

14

homecoming present, was also in the pictures.

Later that day we sat in the paddling pool in her garden. Glenda, a disabled girl from the flats had come round and was in the pool too. Glenda had braces on her legs. I had seen Glenda before but never played with her. We didn't go to her flats and play in the park there because all the kids said that Glenda Jones had got polio from that park. Anyway she had been in hospital when Sharon was there having something done to her legs, and Auntie Maureen had told her mum to bring her over. I thought she was a nice girl. I asked Sharon why she was in the papers, and she said that it was because of her operation. I didn't know what an operation was, but I had heard of it and I knew my sister had had one. When I went home I asked my mother if she had the pictures from when Lizzy was in the papers. My mother looked very puzzled and asked, "Who said that Lizzy was in the papers? She has never been in the papers."

So I continued, "When she had an operation wasn't she in the papers like Sharon?"

She then began to laugh and explained that Sharon's operation was very special, and that Lizzy had only had her tonsils out. I didn't really understand what tonsils were, but I accepted what she said. I was really proud to have a friend who had had a special operation.

Sharon's operation brought changes. She became strong and robust and bossier than ever. Sharon's dog Fifi was lethal. She was a toy poodle, and what she didn't have in size she made up for in viciousness. She was okay with people she knew, but she habitually attacked strangers. They had to stop letting her go out at the front because she always bit someone. The next few years were memorable ones. Our games became quite daring and adventurous. Sharon always persuaded me to do things I knew I wasn't really allowed to do. This included: pinching pick and mix from Arthur's shop and running away, playing knock down ginger, and going off somewhere not in our street when we were supposed to stay outside. Sharon got me into so much trouble all the time. Now that Sharon could run, everything changed.

One of our favourite places to go was a very long apartment block at the end of our street. We loved to run up and down the stairs and along the balconies; past what I thought must be a thousand front doors. One day a woman came out and said, "What are you kids doing here? You don't live here, you live in the cottages. Now clear off!"

There was a certain amount of envy about families who after the war had been housed in the terrace rows which they called cottages. Even at school the other children called us posh and said that we live in the countryside bit of the estate. In the flats opposite, there was a strange little old lady who walked around talking to herself all the time. She always wore the same beige coat and a maroon beret covering her grey hair. You could see little wisps of hair sticking out from beneath the beret. She hobbled around and as well as talking, she often made gestures in the air, such as fist shaking or finger wagging. It was as if she was continually scolding the streets and houses. All the children called her Mary Bagels, because apparently in her younger years she had gone from door to door selling Bagels. She was our favourite victim for playing knock down ginger because she used to chase us and rant and rave. We found it hilarious, until one of the other neighbours who lived in the flats told my mother. Then I was in trouble and banned from playing it. Well it had all been Sharon's idea anyway.

When I was seven, Sharon told me all about sex. I wasn't sure if I believed her. I wondered why people would do something like putting their privates together, and how doing that could make a baby anyway! She also told me what a pro was, and about periods which happen when you are a teenager. Then I knew she was lying. Private parts don't just bleed because you are teenager, not unless you get a cut there. And how would you cut yourself there? She had made it all up. I didn't dare tell her that I didn't believe her though, and I didn't ask my parents or Lizzy if it was true because then I would get into trouble again for being too rude.

The Beatles were all the rage at that time and we talked about them a lot. Lizzy had some of their records and we used to collect pictures of them from newspapers and magazines and we made a scrapbook. Sharon's new game was playing 'going to bed with one of the Beatles and making a baby', but not with Ringo!

Sharon made a best friend at school. Her name was Mavis Rose and she started coming round a lot. Sharon and Mavis were ten now and treated me like a little kid. I was jealous of Mavis. One day I told Auntie Maureen that Sharon had brought Mavis round for a picnic in the garden when she was at work, and that she took food from the larder. In fact my mother provided the sandwiches and cream soda and Sharon had taken very little from her own kitchen. However Sharon got into trouble and didn't talk to me for nearly a week. I also made friends at school and they used to come round. Sharon, was more direct about her jealousy, and told me that she didn't like my best friend Linda, and if I didn't stop being her friend, she wouldn't talk to me anymore. She also told me who I could and couldn't invite to my birthday party and said that she wouldn't come if I invited people whom she didn't like. I did as she said, as always, and made a lot of enemies, often falling out with girls I really liked.

When Sharon was twelve, the family bought a house in Epping. I was very upset, but her house was on the 'Green Line' bus route and I was able to visit sometimes. My parents occasionally drove there to visit Auntie Maureen and Uncle Mike. I loved the new house, in the real countryside. Sharon did horse riding now and one day she took me. It was a real adventure even though I couldn't get up on the horse by myself and had to be lifted up by the teachers. Sharon had made new friends in Epping. There was one girl who had the most beautiful long blond hair I had ever seen. We were not jealous of each other's friends anymore.

Sharon had been born needing major heart surgery. In those days they did not perform such procedures on infants, and if she lived until seven years old she could have it done then. Her lips used to turn blue if she became short of oxygen, which was why they called her a blue baby. Even at seven, Sharon was one of the first children to have an operation like this and survive. This was why she was in the newspapers; she had made pioneering medical history. My mother was right. This had been very special. I think back and realise how brave the family had been. Sharon was their only child and her chances of survival very uncertain. When Sharon was eighteen, they had to be brave again when Maureen battled with cancer and eventually died.

A House of ill Repute

In the days when nobody had coffee mornings as such, but women sat in each other's kitchens almost every day drinking tea or coffee, but mostly tea, gossip was rife.

In our street, Vera gave them plenty to talk about. They always stopped dead if we children came into the house, but we often heard snippets which none of us really understood. We all called her Auntie Vera as we called all the women Auntie. He was Uncle Jack to us, although I don't remember him speaking to me even once. They also had a baby called Lucy, or at least we thought she was their baby. It never occurred to us that they were a different sort of family to everybody else's family.

Baby Lucy cried, often screamed, night after night. I wondered why nobody came like they did if I cried. I never dreamt that nobody was there to pick her up or sooth her.

I caught some of the adults' gossip before they realised that I was there and stopped. My father often said things assuming that I wouldn't know what he meant, and usually I didn't. One comment I picked up was that uncle Jack wasn't Lucy's dad, and wasn't Vera's husband. I wondered why he lived there in that case. One day when the aunts were in Kevin's kitchen, I heard a whole conversation and it was as follows:

"I blame the council, they put him there when he came out. These houses were supposed to be for families with children, not the likes of him!"

"When he first came, he had that girl Rosie with him. Now she was a sweet girl. Very young and not much up top, but sweet all the same. She asked my Ann in for tea once. I wasn't keen but he wasn't there, so she went anyway. She said that Rosie had a record player and loads of records and she played some to her. Ann said they were all classical music and opera. He had probably done over a record shop or something."

19

"Once she knocked at my door and asked me if I had any ideas about what she could cook for Jack's tea that night. So I asked if she had thought about doing mince. Then she asked me how to cook it, and I told her what to do. I even wrote it down but I think she couldn't read. Anyway that night, Mike was in the garden and Jack called across the fence, look at what your wife told my Rosie to cook. He showed Mike a bowl of pale liquid with some bits of meat and veg floating in it! Poor girl, really useless."

"True, she was useless but sweet, but this woman, this Vera, she's as hard as nails and she neglects that child, I mean the whole street can hear it screaming at night."

"Once she left her out in the garden on her own and shut the door. I think she had the men and women in the house. She was leaning over the fence picking all the buds off my peony, and later when I told that horrible Vera about it, she told me to leave her alone she's only a baby! Well a baby shouldn't be left in the garden by herself with nobody watching her."

One afternoon, I was playing in my garden on a hot sunny afternoon. The back door in Vera's house opened and four women emerged wearing swimsuits. They spread towels on the grass and began to lie down. My mother quickly called me into the house and shut our back door. I didn't know why. Another time though mother didn't notice that the women had come out, and Lucy was crawling around on the grass chuckling and burbling, enraptured by her new found freedom. I went to the fence and began laughing with her. Vera came over and started stroking my hair and exalting my cuteness and beauty with the others agreeing. I thought they were nice.

I often saw policemen come to the door, and my father said to my mother one night, "There's plenty of bent coppers ready to take a hand out you know." I had no idea what this meant, I knew that coppers meant pennies, and I knew what a hand was, but that didn't make sense of what he said. If ever I asked, the answer was always the same; it was grown up stuff that I wouldn't understand.

The other thing we saw, was men with square cases going in and out. I overheard Auntie Maureen saying that they were photographers. One evening my father and Uncle Mike, asked Uncle Jack if he could have a word with Vera about the women on the lawn saying that it wasn't good for the children to see. The next morning our doorsteps were littered with things that looked like dark yellow balloons that had been deflated my mother said to Auntie Maureen that it was revenge for complaining.

In spite of all this, when Lucy could walk and talk we played with her. Kevin wasn't allowed to but Sharon and I were as our parents agreed that it wasn't the child's fault. We didn't know what that meant but it was more grown up stuff. Lucy was funny. She liked being tickled and being swung round and liked rolling on the floor. My mother was out one day and my sister Lizzy was looking after me. She was a good dancer and had attended Ballet School from a young age. She used to subscribe to a magazine called Dance and Dancer, which she could only buy from Covent Garden. If she was looking after me, and she wanted to get her magazine, I would go with her. This day Lucy was playing with me and I asked if she could come too. My sister agreed that it would be alright as long as her mum allowed it. So permission obtained, we set out. I loved going on the train. We had to change trains at Kings Cross and go on the escalators. That was fun.

On arrival at Covent Garden, the lifts took us to the street level and then we walked to the news stand outside the big grand white building which was Covent Garden Opera House. I knew it because my sister had taken me to see the ballet Sleeping Beauty. It was so beautiful and I got to meet the ballerina with the long name, which my sister said was a Russian name. Lizzy bought her magazine and then Lucy asked if we could go to the garden now and play. She was most upset when she found out that Covent Garden wasn't a real garden, and she wallowed in disappointment all the way home.

One day they all disappeared. At first I thought they had gone to Spain like Sharon did once, but they never came back again. Then an older lady and man moved into the house, and they were very quiet people. The following year, Sharon showed me a picture of Vera in the newspaper. She was wearing a fur hat and I thought she looked nice. I asked Sharon why Vera was in the papers, and Sharon said to me, "Remember I told you about those pros? You know I told you they take off all their clothes and things, in front of men and get money for it! Well she was one of those and now she's going to prison." I didn't ask my parents because they didn't know that I knew what a pro was, but I asked Lizzy and her friend Kaye. They said that it was true.

I never found out what happened to Lucy.

School Days

I couldn't wait. Every day I asked how many more days there was until school. I would be big like Sharon. Anticipation, excitement and euphoria, mixed together inside my head, and I was like a cloud ready to burst.

The school was a modern building composed of rectangular grey slabs, no doubt riddled with asbestos! The windows were large and adorned the front of the building facing out to a paved area where parents, mostly mothers, delivered and collected. There were no car parks, and no such thing as the school run. We all walked. There were no 'walk to school weeks' to show that we were green. If walking to school was green, we were it and didn't even know it!

In spite of that we still had smog. We called it a 'pea souper' when it was a thick yellow fog. My mother made me wrap a scarf around my face to cover my nose, as we made our way through the yellowy green curtain of air, hardly able to see a foot in front of us.

But this first September day was good, cloudy but still warm and dry. My mother had told me about the road man who stopped the traffic near school so we could cross safely. I imagined a man with huge iron pincers that grabbed the cars and held them in place while we crossed. I was disappointed when I saw the little round lollipop on a stick and wondered how that could possibly stop a car. However, they seemed to stop when he held it up in the road, so it did work.

Road crossed, school was reached. It was on two sites, either side of the yard, where apparently we all played out during the day. Ours was a single storey building which stretched along the entire street. The building across the yard, was a two storey building which was for bigger children like Sharon. Along the back of the yard, was a single storey row which was offices. My father worked in an office but I didn't think it was one of these. I learnt that one of these offices was where you went if you felt sick or had a tummy ache, and a welfare would look after you, whatever that was. Another of the offices was where the teachers had tea whilst we played out. But the most important office was where the lady in charge of the whole school sat, and she was called the Head Mystery. I didn't know why, but thought that perhaps she was never really seen by anyone, so she was a mystery person. On the other side of the offices, was another yard where apparently we had to play out. The big yard was for the older children.

On this day, hordes of mothers and children were gathered outside on the paved area, waiting for the doors to open. Each classroom had a list of children's names posted on the window, so my mother found the correct room and we waited. My excitement grew and grew, as if when the doors opened, I would fly in.

At last the time came. Parents were allowed into the classroom initially to settle their children. I found it odd that many of the children were crying, but I didn't understand that for many of them, it was their first separation from mother. Of course I had grown up with my mother's long hospital stays, so it was nothing to me. In fact, I wanted her to go so that I could get on with school and whatever that entailed. She didn't stay long. I was perfectly happy, so she left me already engrossed with some coloured bricks at one the tables, amidst the hysteria of boys and girls clinging onto their mother's skirts or hanging around their necks sobbing hopelessly, sure that if they let go, it would be forever! But in my experience, mother always came back, eventually.

A few days into the school week, we were given large blank white sheets of paper, and the teacher told us to try and write our names. Lizzy had taught me to do this so I felt really good. She then proceeded to write some words on a large black board using white chalk, and instructed us to copy the words onto our paper. I couldn't do this. I didn't know what she had done, and try as I did, I couldn't look from her board to my paper and reproduce it. I wasn't ashamed at that point, I told all the kids sitting near me that it was too hard so I was going to write my ABC instead. This was another thing that Lizzy taught me. I couldn't keep the letters in a straight line though. Lizzy always gave me paper with lines on and told me to write on the lines, but this paper didn't have any lines. So my ABC resembled a snake, and furthermore the letter size was variable to say the least.

That night, I slept restlessly, terrified that I would be in trouble for not copying the teacher, and writing my ABC instead. She had already smacked one of the boys for being defiant, and I was sure it would be my turn tomorrow. The next day I told my mother that I didn't fancy going to school today, but she told me that I have to go every single day. So for the first time I went into school crying. My mother thought it was a delayed reaction to starting school, and I didn't dare tell her what I had done.

First we played at the tables and the teacher called out names to check that we were there, then we had our milk. The milk was warm with thick cream at the top, and I really didn't like it but I had to drink it. It was part of the school rules. After that the dreaded moment arrived and our teacher was giving us back our writing. I was trembling inside. Everyone was being told that they had done nice writing! The whole class would know that I was the only one who didn't do as I was told, and they would see me chastised. My turn came, "Ellen," she said, still smiling which I found strange. "Your writing was lovely, and you know all your letters! Well done, let's all give Ellen a big clap for knowing her letters!" I turned a shade of crimson and smiled stupidly as the class applauded.

From then on writing became easy. I learnt to read all the books about Janet and John. Every time we finished a book, we got to hold it up in assembly and we got a reward of iced gems from the teacher. Sharon said that it was all very babyish in the infants, particularly the fact that we could sit anywhere we liked in the assembly hall. There was a girl in Miss McBride's class who had very long hair, and everybody tried to sit near her if there was a space.

I learnt to dislike my teacher very quickly. She was young and very tall with sandy coloured shoulder length hair which flicked out at the ends. Her face was quite stern and I found her harsh. She smacked for many reasons, and I tried hard to avoid being smacked. One day we were going to the hall for P.T. We always did P.T. in our vests and pants but it was a cold day and she told us to wear our cardigans to walk to the hall. I didn't hear her. This was probably because I was intent on getting ready quickly. This was my favourite lesson and the quicker we were at getting ready, the longer the lesson.

There were several others who failed to comply with her instruction. She must have been in her element with about eight children to smack. She made us form an orderly queue for the privilege of receiving our corporal punishment. I was at the back of the line. Each child was asked why they had disobeyed and each child said that they weren't cold. Then followed the sound of the slap and the wailing of the child. By the time it got to me, I was already crying. I told the truth and said that I hadn't heard her say it. She looked at me in earnest and said, "Oh well, I'll let you off this time, but you must listen more carefully in future."

Her name was Miss Wicket, and we made up a rhyme, Miss Wicket plays cricket! Then she got married and became Mrs Rolf. So we made another rhyme, Mrs Rolf plays golf! The following year, we had a lovely teacher who didn't smack anybody and she was patient and softly spoken.

Our class was a miss mash of characters. At our tender ages, it didn't occur to us not to like each other or not to accept each other for any reason. Anything we found curious, we asked about, such as why Ted had brown skin. I liked that colour and wondered how he got it like that. Somebody in the class said that it was because he came from another country called Africa. I wondered if I could

26

go there and get skin like that. But when I asked him how far it was to go to the country he came from, he said he came from England, so I had to leave it at that. He became a good friend to me. My mother took a few hours work in the local haberdasher's shop and Ted's mum also worked there, and they became good friends too.

As we got older, use of nicknames became used frequently. A girl joined our class and she was called Teresa Brown, so we called her Trees are Brown. My middle name was Beatrice and they called me Meaty Beatty. Georgina Clark was called Ina after Ina Sharples from Coronation Street on the telly. A girl named Mary Jane Jones joined our class and told us that everyone should call her Koko, as they called her that at home. We didn't know why.

The Infant school day was a mixture of learning, playing and coming together. The latter was my favourite thing, particularly if we did singing. We would all sing together in varying pitches and tones, but nobody cared, we sang our hearts out. We would all sing rhyming ditties led by the teacher, then we would be given the opportunity to stand up alone for a turn. We had few inhibitions and so most hands would go up.

A real class favourite for singing was Mickey Ross. He was a stocky boy with straw coloured hair and a ruddy complexion. He had a gruff, tuneless voice. He always performed the same song, the theme tune from 'Rawhide', which was a cowboy series on the telly. We grinned from ear to ear listening to him belting out, 'Rolling, Rolling, Rolling, keep those doggies moving Rawhide!" and at the end, there would be unanimous applause and laughter. There would also be various renditions of popular songs by Del Shannon, Neil Sedaka, and Doris Day and of course Cliff and Elvis. I liked to sing, 'How Much is that Doggie in the Window'.

I loved playtimes. The Infant yard backed onto the Regents Canal, and I loved standing at the fence, watching people catch fish, and watching the barges go along. I wondered where they were going to, and thought it must be a lovely life driving a boat along the still calm water. We were allowed to take sweets to school for playtime, and we would often sit on the ground in groups and share them.

When we became juniors and moved to the other building, things changed. We did not play in class anymore. Our teacher streamed us in rows according to ability. We learnt very quickly who was clever and who wasn't and prejudice crept in; contempt for those in the lowest row four, and resentment for the clever clogs in row one. I was in the very acceptable row two which meant that I was clever, but not too clever. The teacher actually used the row system as a punishment. I was put in row three one day for talking too much and I was mortified. She was a short matronly woman with long, untidy, mousy hair. She told us that she had come from another country called South Africa. She liked to hit with a ruler, and she liked to humiliate us. One day she sellotaped Annette's mouth up for persistent chatting and she made Gillian kneel at her desk for an afternoon because she was rocking on her chair.

In South Africa, people were segregated by law, and humiliation was an everyday occurrence. Nelson Mandela was in prison for campaigning for the rights of black people to vote and be treated equally to white people. Of course, at the time, I knew nothing of this, or anything about this teacher's beliefs or attitudes, but thinking back I found it ironic that the first person who ever separated us and made us feel different to each other, was a White South African. That same year, a Turkish boy joined our class. His name was Kemour and I thought it was a great name. But for some reason she said that it sounded too different and asked if we would all call him Kenny. So from then on, he was known as Kenny which wasn't nearly as nice as Kemour.

We learnt about prejudice quite thoroughly over the

next few years. A lot of it had come from parents and older siblings I think. The largest ethnic minority group at the time were Jews. In school, it seemed to be okay to be a Jewish boy, so Stephen and Graham were accepted, but Jewish girls were the butt of anti-Semitic jokes and comments. I had Jewish childminders so many of the children assumed that I was Jewish and some of the more unpleasant characters taunted me as part of all this prejudice.

But this aside, most of the time, I was contented at school and I had a wide circle of friends who didn't care what I was or wasn't. I was still friends with Ted and in our last year at primary school, he was sat next to me. We used to play cards under the table during lessons. We played Gin Rummy and Chase the Ace. One day Ted grabbed the ace out of my hand and screwed it up, so I hit him. We inevitable got caught then, and our cards were confiscated. But I liked our teacher Mr Carter. He was always fair.

When I first found out that I was to have a man teacher, I cried. I had always had women teachers and he was a big tall man with a booming voice. However, I soon got over my fears. He taught our class for two years, and I learnt lots. He made everything interesting, and he never skimped on praise for achievement. He was firm, but he tended not to hit or humiliate us. He often told us what we should do rather than what we shouldn't. He played the guitar, and most days ended with a sing along. He seemed to have a fascination for sea shanties and he taught us songs like, 'Blow the Man Down', and 'Johnny Todd'. At Christmas he took us to sing carols at the Royal Festival Hall along with children from lots of other schools. It was wonderful. Then he started a choir, and we performed at a festival in the Peoples Palace Hall in the University. He took the whole class to Epping Forest one Saturday, and we studied trees, plants and wildlife. We were all so excited. He encouraged me to write creatively and to paint. These were two things that I was quite good at, and he told my parents that I had talent. I believe that he was a very skilled teacher and in many ways ahead of his time. In all my years as a teacher, I am not sure that I ever aspired to that level.

I was one of the pupils who passed the eleven plus, so I went to the grammar school. It meant that I was separated from many of my classmates, but have since re-connected with some on social media.

All the Queen's Cars

The whole school went out. It was a lovely day, the sun shone, and it was warm; everything that a summer's day should be. We were marched across the road in orderly lines, two abreast, and on to the top of my street. We lined the pavements. Each of us had been given a little Union Flag on a stick so we could wave it furiously when the time came.

The Queen would be coming along my street, in her car. I had seen pictures of the Queen and I think I had seen her on television. She always wore a long white sparkly dress, with a royal blue cloak trimmed with fur, and on her head she wore an enormous crown, with diamonds and every coloured jewel you could imagine. I couldn't wait to see her in all her finery.

Five year old children had little idea of what a queen's car would look like, and in those days, side roads were not very busy. Several cars came through whilst we waited, and we cheered and waved our flags at all of them. They were all the Queen's cars to us! Most of the bemused occupants of the cars, waved back, and we asked each other if that had been her. The cars passed quickly and I was terrified that we had missed her. I doubt that some of the people knew why they were being cheered, and clearly we had no idea what we were looking for. We seemed to be there for a very long time though.

Then she came. The car was very big, black and shiny. It moved slowly. The Queen was in the back and the window was open. She smiled and waved as she passed by. I cheered with everybody else, but inside I was disappointed and felt cheated. She was wearing a dress and coat, and matching hat. I think the outfit was blue, but can't quite remember. Where was the crown though? Where was the fur and diamonds? Why was the Queen wearing an ordinary suit and hat?

I said very little on the walk back to school, and did not

outwardly share my disappointment that day. I learnt that day, that sometimes the Queen wears ordinary clothes. At home, my mother said that she wouldn't exactly call her clothes ordinary, they were the sort of outfits that she herself might wear to a wedding, although a much less expensive version. Lizzy laughed at me and said that I thought the Queen wore her crown and robes to bed. I hadn't said that at all, and I walked out of the room in a huff.

I saw a re-run of the Queens visit a few months later. My sister Ann sent us a cine film of her baby boy's first birthday party, from Canada. We didn't have a cine projector, so my mother invited Syd and his wife Sadie to our house for the evening. He owned the local draper's shop where my mother and Mrs Green worked part time. They brought their cine projector and screen and we set it up in our front room. We watched the film from Canada, which was hilarious because the baby stuck his whole head in his food bowl and had baby food all over his face. Then we watched Syd and Sadie's holiday film, and at the end of the reel, they had the Queen's visit to our street, in her black car wearing an ordinary suit and a flowery hat, not a crown.

Historically the visit was to show the Queen all housing developments built on the ruins of the East End of London after the blitz. It was to show that the bomb sites were slowly disappearing as building continued. Not too slowly for us though, there were still enough debris for us to play and have fun on.

Illness and How to perform a
Tonsillectomy According to Ali

My mother had a fear about any of us being ill. She had suffered some real scares in the past, such as Ann having diphtheria during the war and then hepatitis later on. Lizzy was a sickly child and she almost died of pneumonia at three years old. I once found Aspirins and ate them, but it turned out that I hadn't taken enough to do any real harm.

We all had childhood illnesses as there were no readily available immunisations for measles, mumps or German measles, so we had them all. Chicken pox was the worst for me as it itched so and the Calamine Lotion, applied to relieve the itching, smelt like mud.

When I was five years old there was a smallpox epidemic and we all had to be vaccinated. The vaccine gave me a fever and the wound turned septic and I became unwell for a while.

But worst of all was my recurring tonsillitis. By the time I was eight years old, I was getting it several times a year. It was common practise to remove tonsils if they were causing a problem, and my mother said that Lizzy had been in much better health once she had them out. So a referral was made and then came the recommendation to have the operation. I was nine by the time I was sent the appointment to have it done. I had no fear, it was a great adventure. The place I was sent to was in Brentwood, Essex. It was part of the Royal London Hospital, but an annex for children. So I was even going on a trip to the countryside.

The ward was full of children. I was going to make new friends. I soon learnt that all the children on the ward were either having tonsils, adenoids, or both removed. There was also a girl who was having her sinuses washed, whatever that meant. I wondered why she needed to be in hospital just to have something washed! There was a boy named Ali on the ward, and I made friends with him quickly, because he liked to joke and play tricks on people. He was a boy of about my age and had black silky hair and darkish skin with blushed cheeks. He told me that he had been born in India, but came to England with his parents when he was a baby. He was full of mischief and had a cheeky smile. He hid other children's things, and he told everyone that the needle they gave you to put you to sleep, was a foot long and they put it in your arm and it came out the other side. He was reprimanded by the ward Sister because he had frightened some of the younger children. But Ali was not easily deterred. The next day he told everyone that when they took out your tonsils, they had to cut off your head, take out the tonsils then stick your head back on with cement. I laughed so much I thought I would burst. Once again, the wrath of the Sister came down on him as some of the children were now crying. I thought that Ali was great and I didn't like the sister anyway, she was sour and always cross like some of the teachers at school. Even my mother said that she was harsh and full of self-importance.

Later on that day, she told us all to tidy the ward because Matron was doing her rounds that afternoon. I asked the others who Matron was, and Ali said that she was in charge of the whole hospital and she ate the children who were not good when she came to the ward. However, Matron was an elderly lady who was softly spoken and kind.

There were other nurses who were kind as well. There was one nurse called Nurse Adams, and she wrinkled her eyes when she smiled, which was most of the time. I loved it when she was there. Some nurses were a bit like sister and never smiled.

The third day in hospital was my operation day. I was given a little needle in my bottom that made me feel dreamy. Then I was given one in my hand and the next thing that seemed to happen was that I woke up. I felt very groggy and had a sore throat. The girl who had had the washing whatever it was, was in the next bed being very sick. I slept on and off for the rest of the day, even when my parents visited.

The next day we were allowed to eat ice cream. My throat still hurt and I didn't feel like eating much, not even ice cream. I could feel a lump at the back of my throat, but the doctor said that it would soon go away. Then came the day we were all going home, and I still had the lump. I sat up in bed, had some corn flakes with hot milk then I coughed. I felt the lump move and suddenly a deluge of blood came pouring from my throat. A nurse came running with a bowl, and soon there were several nurses and a doctor at my bedside. I was cleaned up and given another injection.

I didn't go home that day, but when I woke up the lump had gone. Apparently, the lump had been a clot and when it dislodged, it caused something called a secondary haemorrhage. I stayed in hospital for another week and had to take iron tablets because the blood loss had caused anaemia. They were tiny round sugar coated pills, and didn't look anything like iron and I suppose anaemia was some kind of illness that I had got from the lump in my throat.

It meant that I got to see the smiley nurse lots more, and to my delight, Ali had to stay in hospital as well. I didn't know why but perhaps the cement hadn't dried properly when they stuck his head back on. One day Ali went out with his parents and was gone for a long time. When he came back, I asked him where he had been, and he said that he had been to the cricket fields. When my parents came to visit, I asked them to take me to the cricket fields. A girl who had been admitted two days previously, and seemed to know everything, piped up and said that we weren't allowed outside the hospital grounds. It so happened that Matron was doing her rounds at that time, and my mother asked her if they could take me for a walk. Matron said that it would do me good to get some fresh air and my mother added that I had wanted to go to the cricket fields but I wasn't allowed off hospital grounds.

Then Matron kindly said that the cricket fields were on hospital grounds, and directed us on how to get there.

It was just a field and there were men in white trousers and shirts, playing cricket. But I felt triumphant. I had beaten the know it all girl, and I could talk about the cricket fields with Ali because I had been there as well. It was a beautiful warm sunny afternoon, perfect for a walk.

On our return, Sister was on the ward looking very cross. She had asked where I was, and Know it All girl had told her that I had gone to the cricket fields. Sister was a formidable woman who thought nothing of scolding my parents as if they were naughty school children. Naturally my father had a little laugh at the absurdity of it all, but my mother listened calmly. The complaint seemed to be that they had taken me out without notifying anybody of obtaining permission.

My mother looked her in the eyes and said, "Actually we asked Matron and she gave us permission!" So the Sister quietly grumbled that she shouldn't have!

At the end of the week, I was allowed to go home. My adventure had come to an end. I was quite sorry to leave my favourite smiley nurse, and funny, playful, mischievous Ali. My mother spoilt me when we got home. I had a new Sindy doll and my favourite dinners all weekend.

My mother told me that she had spoken to Ali's parents, and that Ali was going to have to stay at the hospital for a long time. The doctors had discovered that there was something seriously wrong with him and he needed lots of treatment. I was very sad and hoped that they could make him better, like they had made Sharon better.

It was many years before I was ill again, but I thought of Ali from time to time and wondered if he was better now.

A Bucket of Piss

I did have real aunts and uncles and lots of them too. My mother's family all lived in places where we had to go by car if we visited; but we could walk to where my dad's sisters lived. My Auntie Ethel and Uncle Jim lived at the end of our street and across the road. They didn't have any children but I visited them often because my Granddad also lived there. My other Aunties Meg and Rose lived in King Street which took about ten minutes to walk to. Auntie Rose and Uncle Tom had one son and he was grown up, but Auntie Meg and Uncle Ralph had six children, my cousins. The youngest, Sue, was two years older than me, and I used to love playing with her.

The houses in King Street were really amazing. They seemed to go on for ever. The ground floor consisted of: a large room at the front, a smaller room behind it, and alongside a passageway which led to a sort of galley kitchen and a small utility room at the back. Outside was a small concrete yard, which led to the only toilet in the entire house. On the first floor were two fairly large rooms and a box room. On the second floor there were more rooms, but I never went up there because Sue's room was on the first floor. She shared her room with my cousin Christine who was three years older than her and very bossy. The two older sisters Jane and Peggy shared the other room on that floor and the two boys were married and lived somewhere else now. I used to think this house was really exciting with all the rooms and stairs. The only thing I didn't like was going to the toilet in the winter or in the dark. The stone floors throughout the ground level were very uneven and were partially covered with some rather worn rugs. The furniture had seen better days in most cases but it was clean and homely and I always felt that it was a bit like the story I knew called, 'The House that Jack Built.'

37

When Cousin Peggy got married, we were all bridesmaids: Jane, Christine, Sue, Lizzy and I. It was so exciting, Sue and I were the youngest and we wore little white laced fairy dresses with lots of netting beneath the skirt to make it stick out like a ballet dancer's dress. We wore flower rings on our heads and carried posies of yellow flowers. The older girls all had satin dresses which didn't stick out like ours and I didn't think they were nearly as pretty. Peggy looked beautiful. I thought that she must be the most beautiful girl in the whole world and that hers was the best dress I had ever seen. The skirt stuck out so much that it looked like a giant silk lampshade. I thought she must have had a hundred layers of net underneath as it cascaded down to the floor and into a train at the back. She wore a pearl tiara and a lace veil which fell around he shoulders to meet the satin bodice of her dress. She carried a huge bouquet of yellow flowers.

Peggy and John (her new husband) moved into the second floor of Auntie Meg's house and the box room was converted into a small kitchen. Sue, Jane and Christine moved up to the second floor so that Peggy and John could have a bedroom and a sitting room on the first floor. The room upstairs was huge. There were two double beds as well as wardrobes and draws and ottoman type chests. This became my favourite room in the house. The other room up there belonged to my aunt and uncle but I don't think I ever went in there in my whole life.

It was a long way from this room to the outside toilet, and not very safe to negotiate the stairs and the uneven floors in the dark. So they had a bucket in the room in case they needed the toilet during the night. It was stored under the bed and emptied in the mornings.

When I was old enough to cross roads on my own, at about eight years old, my mother sent me to Sunday school at the local church. I thought it was boring but it was just across the road from King Street. So when I finished I would go straight to Auntie Megs and stay there until it was time to go home for Sunday dinner. Sometimes I stayed at Auntie Megs for dinner as well. Sue usually slept in and when I got there I would go straight to her room, often waking her up. One morning I went bounding into the room yelling, "Wake up lazy bones!" and ran straight into the bucket which Sue had obviously forgotten to push under the bed. It went everywhere; on the rug, up the side of the bed, over me and a stream ran under the bedstead. Sue was howling with laughter as I screamed in distress. Auntie Meg came running upstairs, as she had heard the commotion two floors up from the kitchen. "What's going on up here?" she cried, quite angrily for Auntie Meg who hardly ever got angry when I was there. Sue was almost choking from laughing, but managed to get the words out, "Ellen's kicked the bucket of piss over." I didn't know whether to laugh or cry. I didn't know what Auntie Meg would do or say, but she became very purposeful and calmly said, "Sue get up. Both of you downstairs now while I clean this mess up." We both obeyed immediately and Sue left the room still giggling and I left sheepishly apologising over and over.

Sue was not supposed to swear, none of us were. If Auntie Meg hadn't been so taken aback by the whole bucket incident, and so keen to get it cleaned up, I think Sue may have got a smack for saying piss. In the summer, we all went to Clacton on sea for a holiday. We stayed in caravans which were on a permanent site and could be hired by holidaymakers. I stayed in the same caravan as my parents and Lizzy, but Auntie and Uncle had to get two caravans, as Peggy and John were also with them. They had all travelled by train but we had a car. It was a black Austin Sunbeam and my Father could drive, so we drove down and met them on the camp site. Lizzy and I sang Beatles songs all the way down and of course I said, "Are we there yet?" a hundred times. The site was separated from the beach by only a dusty track, and we were just dying to get to the sand and paddle in the sea.

At one end of the site there were two blocks of changing rooms one for men and one for women. These contained toilets, rows of wash basins and a communal changing area with wooden benches. On the first afternoon we had sandwiches to eat which my mother had made for both families as we could carry them down in the car. I was slow at eating mine so the other girls all grabbed their towels and bathing suits and went to the changing rooms without me. I protested and then said I was full up but my mother was having none of it. She made me finish my lunch and then let me go to join the others. I ran across the camp full of excitement, through the eggshell blue door of the changing block and stopped in my tracks. I felt my face flush with heat as a grown up man turned his head and stared at me from in front of a urinal, where he was obviously still in full flow. In my excitement I had gone into the men's. I felt really embarrassed and quickly turned around shutting the door behind me, hoping nobody else noticed.

When I got to our changing rooms, the older girls had changed and Sue was moaning because nobody was helping her, and she couldn't get her jersey over her head. So Christine, when ready herself, ran over to her mumbling about all the fuss she was making and yanked the jersey over her head quite roughly. This obviously hurt because Sue yelled out, "Sod it!" Christine smacked her across the back and told her not to swear. There was a mean streak in me I think, because I couldn't wait to tell. I ran outside just as Auntie Meg was coming across the dirt track with my mother, and shouted at the top of my voice, "Sue said Sod it." But all that happened was that I got into trouble for saying it and then Sue came out saying, "I didn't say that, I said sobbin." Then Sue and I started dancing around in a circle singing, "Sobbin robin sobbin robin," over and over.

We built sandcastles, paddled in the sea and found rock pools in the craggy outlets as the rocks met the sea. We had a wonderful week but it went by so quickly.

I think I gave Sue quite a hard time and thinking back, wondered why she put up with me. One of my favourite tricks was telling any kids who upset me that I would get my cousin Sue to fight them. Some of them took me at my word and turned up at her door. She had no intention of ever fighting my battles for me so I often ended up looking pretty stupid!!!

One Sunday morning, I went to Aunt Meg's after church and Sue had a friend sleeping over. When I went into the bedroom, they were in fits of giggles. I had no idea what they had been laughing about, but laughing is contagious and in no time I was giggling too. They then started tickling each other under the arms and I thought it would be great to join in. I made a rush towards the bed and kicked over the bucket of piss again!

Dead Flies and Fried Ants

My father's brother Ben, worked for Breweries. First he worked for Truman in London, and then for McMullen in Hertfordshire. With his jobs, there came tied houses, and the one in Hertford was particularly lovely. I loved visiting Uncle Ben and Aunt Glad. It was usually on a Saturday afternoon because we stayed late but didn't have to worry about school the next day. The house was large, well there were four children, my cousins of course.

There was a large kitchen, a dining room and a lounge. There was a back porch which led to a downstairs toilet and a very long garden. The downstairs toilet had a very funny toilet roll holder. It said:

> **£2500 may come your way**
> **but don't sit here and dream all day!**

The whole day was always very exciting. Lizzy and I always sang in the back seat of my father's old Austin Sunbeam car. We sang Beatles, Hollies, Jerry and the Pacemakers and Cliff Richard songs, all the way to Hertford. We had to drive through Tottenham on a shopping afternoon and it was always very slow traffic. If Spurs were playing at White Hart Lane, it was even worse. I would become impatient and start saying, "Are we there yet?" One day my father answered, "Not far until we reach the dual carriage way."

With the noise of the engine, and the traffic, I misheard him and thought he said the George Harrison Way! "Where's the George Harrison Way?" I asked with delight. The entire family were heaving with laughter, and even now I refer to the Great Cambridge Road as the George Harrison Way! There were landmarks which told me when we were getting close to my uncle's house. One was a garden centre with a windmill, and soon after that we turned onto a country lane, which I named Windly Lane, because it had lots of bends. That led straight to Hertford and our destination.

My cousin Sylvia was three years older than me but we enjoyed playing together. Tom was three years younger than me but he always joined our games. The two older boys Peter and Patrick were more Lizzy's age. If it was good weather, we played in the garden, but on rainy days we played somewhere in the house. Uncle Ben had built a drinks bar in the lounge, and we could play cafes.

Sylvia and I liked to sing popular songs and change the words. Mary Well's song My Guy, we changed to Mud Guy. If you could sing the whole song without laughing, you were the winner.

Uncle Ben was very good at making things. He had made the drinks bar but also some beautiful tall ships in bottles which decorated the lounge. Aunt Glad was a good cook. We always had salad for tea, but she made wonderful cakes. There was usually a Victoria sponge, iced fairy cakes, a walnut and coffee cake which was my mother's favourite and a fruitcake baked in a loaf tin. Uncle Ben always went for the fruitcake and cut himself a slice. He would then say to my father, "Harry, want some G1098?" Apparently this was the serial number given to fruitcake rations when they were in the army, during the war. I still call fruitcake G1098!

My favourite part of the visit was always the evening. The grownups would go to the pub and leave us to our own devices. The oldest cousin Patrick, was in charge, but he didn't mind us playing silly romp around games as long as we didn't break anything. So we would go a bit crazy. One time when we were there, Aunt Glad's sister and her family had visited. Tom was five at the time and so was his visiting cousin Philip. The two of them were playing wrestling, which really consisted of rolling around on the carpet and whacking each other with cushions. Then they had a stand up confrontation over whose dad was the strongest. Ben started, "My dad weighs fifty gallons!" Then Philip came back with, "So my dad weighs eighty gallons." And so it continued until both dads were weighing hundreds of gallons!!

We were always allowed a drink of orange juice or lemonade, and crisps or biscuits. Peter brought in the biscuit tin and presented it to each of us to take some. I had never seen these type of biscuits before. "What are they?" I asked. "Garibaldis," said Lizzy. "What are those black bits in them?" I carried on. Patrick then said that they were dead flies and he wouldn't eat them. Then Peter took one and bit into it. "They're not dead flies, they're fried ants, niiice!!!" I still didn't fancy them after that.

As it got quite late, the time would approach for the adults to return, and we were aware that we needed to be calmer, and put back the cushions and antimacassars which we had thrown around. Then we would listen with one ear whilst continuing with some calmer but equally daft antics. Any noise we heard, someone would say, "Is it them?" "No it's not them," someone else would say, then another noise and, "It's them, quick it's them!"

We would leave shortly after the return of the adults and I often fell asleep in the car.

We all grew up and my cousins married. Peter moved to Hong Kong, and Tom went to University and then married after graduation. Uncle Ben died when I was seventeen, and Aunt Glad had to leave the tied house. The Brewery were very good to her though and found her a small cottage nearby where she lived until moving into sheltered accommodation.

When Aunt Glad died, I was unable to get leave from teaching to attend the funeral. My husband went in my stead, and my cousins told him that he was the only person there to represent their father's family. I was grateful that he went.

When I was small, Uncle Ben had given my father a bottle opener. It was a brass statue of a naked lady. The

44

brewery were giving them as souvenirs for some kind of anniversary. I still have the bottle opener and use it all the time. It is one of my treasured possessions from my early memories.

McMullen's Brewery

Days at the Races

My maternal Aunt Mary lived in Epsom in Surry. She lived in a cul-de-sac with a shingle road, not built for cars but more than likely horses. At the bottom of the road was a turnstile and large gates, leading onto Epsom Downs. If you climbed the hill to the top, you were overlooking Epsom Racecourse.

Every August bank holiday Monday, it was a family tradition to meet up on the hilltop, with my mother's sisters and brothers and their families. We would all make our way up the hill, carrying deckchairs, windbreaks, picnic baskets, and rugs to spread on the grass, footballs and various toys to play with. The downs would be crowded along the top of the hill, and we congregated amongst a sea of people, countless bookmaker's stands, ice cream vans, portable toilets, and knick-knack pedlars and of course gypsies selling heather and horse shoes for good luck. All of us children were given a little money to spend on whatever we wanted. This was our annual family day at the races.

It was exciting because there were so many cousins to play with, and furthermore, the atmosphere was wonderful. It was busy and bustling. There was constant calling from the bookies, shouting the odds and chalking up and rubbing out as they frequently changed. Children ran in and out of the clusters of camps set up by many extended families, who did the same as us, often chased by yapping dogs, as family pets came too. If one of the aunts bought an ice cream for her children, she brought for all of us. I remember feeling quite sick sometimes from too many sweets, crisps and Ninety Nines, which were ice cream cones with two flakes. My mother would tell me not to be so greedy and to slow down.

I loved betting. I could put one shilling on a horse with a pretty name, and win three shillings or even five if I was really lucky. I never knew which horse had won but watching them bolt past, was really thrilling. On the telly, the horses always seemed to move quite slowly, but here, they were like lightning, and the noise of the hooves was like guns firing rounds and rounds. All I could see was dust as they sped by, and all around people were screeching come on to their chosen horses. I always had to show my ticket to a grown up and ask if I had won anything.

One year my father brought his dad, my grandfather along with us. He was very old. He used to visit us every Sunday morning, and go to the pub with my parents. He didn't know any of our names, but he had an awareness of where we should be. So he would always ask, "Where's the big gel, in the bathroom?" and, "What about the little one, gorn a church? How's the one that's away?" He meant my sister Ann in Canada, and my mother always said that it made her sound like she was in prison!

He showed that he also liked betting, as he seemed to bet on every race. He kept saying that he was putting five shillings on Lester. I had no idea what that meant, but he kept winning so I decided that I would put a shilling on Lester. I went to the nearest stand and handed my shilling to the man and said Lester, only to be told that Lester wasn't in this race. So I chose a horse called Rainbow and I won three shillings.

After the races had finished, we would all pack up our things and trundle down to Aunt Mary's house. It was only a small house, but we would all congregate on her long front lawn. The small front parlour would be empty, but the kitchen behind it was a hive of activity, with all the women hard at work, shelling boiled eggs, making salads and sandwiches with a variety of fillings. The kitchen opened onto a small back yard and an outhouse which I hated going to because unlike Aunt Megs outhouse, this was in the country and had many more spiders.

How Aunt Mary fed us all I don't know, but she did, every year. There was always lemonade and cream soda for the children, the ladies drank tea, and the men had beer.

My mother was the second from youngest sibling in her family, and because she was forty when she had me, the family generations were slightly out of sync. Some of my first cousins had grandchildren of my age. Cousin Teddy had a son Jim who was a year older than me. My mother loved Teddy. He was a small man and he had suffered from polio when he was a child. There was a girl named Glenda who lived near us and she had to wear leg braces because she had polio. Teddy's wife Doreen, was much taller than him, and she had a very loud gruff voice. My mother said that she was common and crude and she didn't know why Teddy had chosen her to marry. My mother tended to be quite snobbish and judgemental. Jim was ten, and he was allowed to have a glass of beer. My mother thought it was terrible, and certainly didn't know that Jim had let me have a swig. It wasn't as nice as lemonade so I didn't ask for another. Then Doreen shouted very loudly, "Come on Jim, drink that beer, we have to get going!"

My mother looked at my father and raised her eyebrows, obviously outraged by the whole thing.

The following year, I turned ten, and off we went again to the races on the bank holiday. It was during this year, at that event, that I made a discovery about myself.

My mother's family were an interesting mix. Rumour has it that their mother Eleanor, had been from gypsy stock. She died when my mother was nine, and this, and what followed after, was probably the main cause of her mental health issues later in life. Two of my mother's sisters died when I was quite small, but I remember them as being jovial women who were loving and kind. Aunt Mary, whom we descended upon every year for this event, was a gentile lady, well-spoken and lady like. She had married a man of German descent who had left her, for another woman, with four small sons to bring up alone. The family often referred to him as a bad egg. Then there was Aunt Nellie! She was born Christina Eleanor, but took the name Eleanor because it had been her mother's name. I was also named for my mother's mother and Lizzy for my father's mother. Every one shortened Christina Eleanor to Nellie, and she was such a character. Aunt Nellie used to swear. The story was, that it was a rebellion against their father who was very strict, an ex-army colonel, and he abhorred bad language. So she used it all the time whenever he was out of hearing range, and now it had become natural to her. Her own children who were now grown up, tried to modify her language in front of the children, but it didn't really work.

I thought that she was hilarious. I didn't dare copy her because I wasn't allowed to swear at all, well not in front of my parents anyway. I loved Aunt Nellie, and so did my mother. I could never understand why she moaned about Doreen's language, when her own sister's was even worse.

This particular year, after our usual day at the races, and tea at Aunt Mary's house, everyone decided to come back to our house in Stepney. There were several cars to pile into, and I opted to go in the car with Aunt Nellie, Uncle George, their son Kenny and daughter Nell. Of course, I did this because I wanted to hear her swear! She didn't disappoint either, in spite of young Nell scolding her continually for her language in front of me. The journey from Epsom to Stepney was quite long in those days, and involved crossing London Bridge and driving through the City of London and Aldgate. On reaching that latter, Aunt Nellie had a brainwave. "Let's stop at Tubby Isaacs and get jellied eels," she said.

I had never had jellied eels, but I knew that my mother liked them and so did many people. We parked the car on the corner of Middlesex Street and scrambled across to Tubby Isaac's eel stall.

A vagrant man crossed the road behind us and Aunt Nellie nudged her husband and said, "Well would you fucking believe it, look it's yer father!"

Young Nellie poked her in the back and said crossly, "Mother behave yourself!"

I was bent double laughing. We ordered jellied eels all

round and a tub to take back to my mother. They came with little wooden spoons, and my Aunt was so eager to taste hers that she dropped some down her front and exclaimed, "Fuck it's gorn down me chitters!" Young Nell gave her a disapproving glance and shook her head in despair.

So I was about to embark on a new experience. I took a mouthful of the slippery grey contents and began to chew. It was to be my first and last ever. I found them disgusting. I didn't like the taste or texture. I thought they were horrible. The rest of them were more than happy to polish off my leftovers, and then we carried on our journey. And that was the day I discovered that I don't like jellied eels.

Latch Key Life

We were in one of those old fashioned pubs with flock wallpaper yellow from years of tobacco staining, and worn leather seats which had seen better days. There were six of us, three couples in fact, all with weddings planned within the next two years. Jack had just bought a round and we carried on our conversation, about our work, house hunting and wedding plans.

Jack's girlfriend couldn't wait to sample wedded bliss and to be a stay at home mother for the rest of her life. But my ideas were very different. I didn't want children, I wanted to further my career, travel as a couple and get everything in the home we both wished for. We clashed because we judged each other. I saw her as a person of limited thinking, not being a graduate like the rest of us, and she saw me as being selfish and materialistic, and a bit of a slob because I didn't iron bedsheets!

She worked as an assistant in a day nursery and we had embarked on a conversation about her work. All was fairly amicable until she managed once again, to strike a nerve. She expressed how sorry she felt for the children at the nursery, and I asked her why she felt that way. She gave me her opinion.

"These parents put their kids in day care so they can go off to work, make money and buy lots of clothes and things. If they don't want to look after their kids they shouldn't have them."

I thought about my father, and how he had no choice but to leave me in a nursery, even though I didn't like it. She continued, "I remember when I was at school, and some of the poor kids came in with their front door keys on a string around their neck. We called them 'latch key kids' and we all knew that they had to go home to an empty house while their parents worked. Well my mum stayed at home and looked after me properly!"

"Some people don't have a choice," I said, "Wouldn't

you agree?"

"If they didn't insist on buying all the best things, and all the latest toys for their kids, and the lasted fashions in clothes, mums wouldn't need to work. I didn't have all that stuff, but I had a hot meal waiting for me every night when I got home, and I that's what my children will get because I know what's more important."

I wondered why she carried on doing a job where she continually felt depressed at the plight of those she was caring for.

"Well I was a 'latch key kid', and I was in day care," I told her.

That gave her ammunition to go on and tell me that she now understood why I didn't want children. I was insecure because of my upbringing, and would find it hard to bond with children and form close relationships if I had them.

I bit my bottom lip and took a side glance at Eileen who was keeping her lips tight shut, both of us trying not to show our amusement at this absurd viewpoint. Graham changed the subject on looking from myself to Eileen, it was definitely time!

***

Latch key life was fun. I was never restricted from bringing friends home, at lunch time or after school. I was never short of my peers wanting to come, after all who wouldn't want to come and play in a house where there were no grownups?

Jackie from the flats across the road, used to come and play ghosts. We would close the thick green velvet curtains blocking out all the light, and play ghost hunting. It was really just hide and seek in the dark. Then we liked to play ghost horses. Jackie would crawl around the furniture with me on her back. We always put on Lizzy's record, 'Little Red Rooster' by the Rolling Stones, because we found the bluesy sound quite ghostly. We would sing along to it mimicking the twangy guitar riffs.

When Koko from the big flats came round we played shows. We put on my parents records, My Fair Lady and West Side Story, and sing and dance. The sofa was the pretend audience, and the hearth rug the stage. I was always the woman singer and Koko had to put on a deep voice and be the man.

Jill from The Old Road used to like dressing up. Lizzy was at college training to be a teacher. She stayed at college because it was in Eastbourne, but most of her clothes were at home, in her wardrobe. We used them for dressing up. I had to watch the time, because if my parents came home and caught us, I would be in trouble. One day however, I lost track of time. Jill had put on Lizzy's best dress. It was a very fashionable one, smock shaped with swirling psychedelic patterns in bright colours. It had come from Carnaby Street, and had been modelled by Twiggy. Now Jill was modelling the dress, and I heard the key turn in the door. There was no place to hide, so I quickly made her put on her coat, and stuff he own dress up the sleeve. I flushed the toilet, so it appeared that Jill had been in there before leaving for home, and then we both ran downstairs Jill said goodbye and left.

So Jill went home wearing Lizzy's best dress mouthing that she would bring it to school tomorrow. I tidied my school desk in the morning to hide the dress, but Jill didn't bring it. She was very flustered and began telling me a worrying story. She talked so fast that she scarcely drew breath. On the way home, she realised that she couldn't go indoors wearing the dress, so she had gone into the toilets in Shady Park and changed. She hid the dress in some bushes at the back of her flats where nobody ever goes. Her Idea was to retrieve the dress next morning, but inevitably it had gone.

I didn't mention it at home. If Lizzy wasn't there, nobody would miss the dress. But six weeks later Lizzy was home for a holiday, and one night she was going somewhere special and wanted to wear the dress. It wasn't in the wardrobe and she searched the house looking for it.

I said nothing, but my mother was looking at me with suspicious eyes thinking that I probably knew something. She thought about who had been in the house with me. She knew that Sharon or Kevin wouldn't have taken it, but wasn't so sure about Jackie, Koko or Jill. So she began ringing their parents asking if they had seen the dress. They were quite upset that my mother was suggesting that their child may have stolen something. Jill's parents came round to discuss the whole thing and neither of us said a word!

So the event remained a mystery, and I lost friends for a while until it was all forgotten.

The friends who came home with me at lunchtime, shared my squash and sandwiches which mother had left for me, but I didn't always come to the house. So that my parents wouldn't know, we would eat the sandwiches after school. Sometimes, we went to the fabric factory in Copperfield road. They would leave out scraps of fine materials in large sacks outside the large entrance shutters. We would raid the sacks and collect: satin, velvet, lace, silk and gold glittery material. Then we could make party and wedding dresses for our Sindy dolls. Our teacher used to let us use some of our sewing classes to continue making them, and one afternoon we had a class competition displaying all our dolls. I had seven Sindy dolls, but Koko had dolls from all over the world, in National Costumes, and so she won.

One day Ghostly Jackie, when she was friends with me again, asked me to go with her to get pie and mash over the iron bridge. I had never had pie and mash before, so I said that I would come. I had a little bit of pocket money with me, but she said we could share anyway. Then Hazel, a girl with two long plaits in her hair, tied at the back, said that she had money and wanted to come. So we set off along the road to the iron bridge and across the grass to the main road. I told them that I had never had pie and mash before. Both girls looked astonished. They had never heard of anybody who hadn't ever had pie and mash. They assured me that it tasted wonderful and that I would love it.

As we approached the shop, there was a bit of a queue, but we had lots of time. As we opened the door however, a smell hit me. It seemed to me a pungent, rancid smell. It reminded me of the smell of the dinner hall at school. This odour was the reason I refused to stay for school dinner. It smelt like old brown stew and over boiled cabbage. Then we were nearly at the front of the queue, and I saw it. A man in front had got his and I blurted out, "What's that green stuff?"

"Oh replied Hazel, that's the liquor, you've got to have the liquor."

"It looks like snot!" I said.

"Tastes lovely," she said.

Then it was our turn to be served. They both ordered pie and mash. The man looked at me and I said, "Have you got anything else?"

"Jellied eels," he replied, "And lemon ice."

So I had a delicious tub of lemon ice, and they had old brown stew in a soggy pie, with lumpy grey mashed potatoes, all covered in snot!

I remained a latch key kid, until I became a latch key teenager and a latch key adult. I became quite an accomplished cook, as I prepared the evening meals for myself and my parents. So they arrived home to a hot meal every night, and they were grateful for it.

Debris

Health and safety measures would ensure that we couldn't gain access to these places nowadays. There would be boarding and padlocks and danger warnings, and probably quite rightly so. These were very unhygienic and dangerous places. But to us, they were: playgrounds, wild gardens, treasure troves, camps and dens. We loved the World War II bomb sites, and they were abundant. There was one opposite my infant school, one at the end of my road, one near Aunt Meg's house and my favourite one near the iron bridge.

Image from the Guardian.

To my mother's despair we played on them all. The one opposite school, was brilliant for picking wild flowers. There were: poppies, mallow, cowslip, feverfew, meadowsweet and many more. I used to pick them and take a posy home. I never picked dandelions because Sharon said that they made you wet the bed! Of course there were nettles and thistles to avoid, but I often got stung. Then I would have to have calamine lotion and would be told to stop going on the debris.

During my second year at school, the debris was levelled and prefab houses were built. They were funny little houses I thought. The reminded me of the caravan parks at Clacton and Maldon. But there were rows and rows of them, all identical shiny white and yellow panels with black edging. They were the ultimate Lego houses.

The best debris for building a den was the one near the iron bridge. It was a bombed out pub and the bottom was at cellar level. Therefore, it was necessary to climb down and it was a perilous climb. I was often bruised and cut and of course filthy by the time I reached the bottom. I went there with ghostly Jackie and the two Stephens from my class. We used some old chairs, and stacked some crates to make the walls, then we draped some damp rotting curtains, covered in mildew across the top to make a roof. There were always mattresses lying around which we could use a flooring. I spiked myself on a broken spring which was protruding from a large tare in the mattress. The sharp metal hidden by course stuffing also protruding. So I returned home with a gash in my leg and got into trouble for playing on the debris yet again.

The day after this event, as I left for school, my mother said, "Don't you dare go on the debris." And I replied solemnly, "No mum I won't."

As soon as school had finished, I found the two Stephens outside the gates, and asked who was coming to the debris. Only one of the Stephens could come and Jackie was away from school, so we set off together. To our delight, our den was still there untouched. I was very careful not to get too dirty climbing down. Stephen had some penny chews, Spanish laces and milk bottles in his pocket so we sat in our damp, smelly den eating sweets.

Then I saw it. It was the biggest beetle I had ever seen, and it had horns. I screamed and ran out pulling half the curtains down with me and knocking over the crates. In my rush to escape from the crawling monster, I fell over some rubble, grazed my other leg and dirtied my clothes in the process. I had to face the wroth of both my parents as it was quite obvious where I had been.

I decided not to go back to that debris and thought I might try the one at the end of my street. I bribed Jackie and the Stephens with crisps and sweets, and they abandoned the iron bridge debris for the one on my street. I was taking a risk, as this was an open site and could be seen by passers-by. So if Lizzy or my parents happened to pass, I would be caught. Lizzy didn't usually come home from school that way she walked through the flats, but my parents did, and so I had to watch the time.

This debris was not very interesting, there was only bricks and rubble, nothing to make a den with. So the others lost interest and didn't want to play there anymore.

One day, I decided to go back to the iron bridge and brave the giant beetles. I went alone to see if our den was still there. It had been a few weeks but the remnants of the dwelling were still evident. I began to look for bits to build it up properly again. But I uncovered a horror which was to cure me of my compulsion to visit these unsavoury playgrounds for good.

I moved a large piece of dark blue taffeta curtain, which seemed to be quite clean and would make a great roof, from a pile of rubble. Underneath the material, laid a large black dead dog. The putrid odour made me retch. Yellow puss oozed from its orifices and a huge gash in the belly, from where the stinking guts spilled out, was alive with wriggling, writhing maggots. I didn't panic, I made my way to the wall and carefully climbed to the top of the staggered brick work, never to return.

That debris shortly after, became a building site, and some council flats were built there. When King Street was demolished, Aunt Meg moved into some high rise flats, but then some years later into the flats on this site. The debris at the end of our street, was levelled and a Fish and Chip shop built. When my mother found out what was going to be there she complained bitterly, saying that the whole street would smell of fish and fat. It didn't though, and Fish and Chips from the new shop became a Friday night favourite at home.

© The Local Data Company

Trouble Over Soup

When Lizzy turned fifteen, my mother was anxious that she should have a bedroom of her own, so my mother applied for a house exchange. Mrs Rust had passed away, and the house was occupied by just Alan and his wife Marge. The young couple wanted a smaller house with two bedrooms and we wanted three. So the council arranged a straight swap between us and everybody was happy. Lizzy and I had a room each, and if Ann visited from Canada, we could double up just for a short period.

The new house was in the next row and was next to the road, rather than being set back like the old house. Both houses were at the ends of the terrace, so really, it was only next door, we were moving from number 35 to 36. It was fun moving all our goods from one house to the other. Alan and Marge helped my parents to move the heavy goods, and we ran back and forth with the lighter goods. Kevin and Sharon helped as well. However when it was all done, and we were in, I began to feel rather upset. I cried in bed that night wanting my old house back. The next day I felt much better and I played out with Sharon and Kevin.

We had new neighbours. Mrs Jacobs who was an elderly widow, lived next door in number 37. Next to her was a lady called Rosa but we didn't really know her at first, but next in the row was Auntie Mary and Uncle Isaac. They had two older children, teenagers like Lizzy, and their names were Ruth and Josh. Ruth was Lizzy's friend. Ruth said that when they were younger, they used to do plays and dancing on the grass squares along with Kaye and Rosa's girl Myra. They would entertain all the neighbours and passers-by. Uncle Isaac's sister also lived with them, and her name was Auntie Golda.

They were a Jewish family and were long standing friends of my parents. They had all been neighbours before they moved to our street. They also used to look after me when I came home from school and they were at work, and I loved going in their house. Auntie Mary used to give me chopped liver or chopped herring on Matzo and I found it delicious. Sometimes, I would watch her boil chickens and make her wonderful Kreplach Soup. I loved Jewish food.

Then they bought a puppy, a black Labrador named Sheba. She was lively and cute. At first I loved her, but as she grew bigger and bigger, I wasn't so sure. One night, I had a bad dream that Sheba was chasing me and I couldn't escape. She was barking furiously and looking fierce. I was terrified of Sheba and wouldn't go to Auntie Mary's house any more. So Auntie Golda had to come to my house and sit with me until my parents got home. This went on until my parents deemed it safe for me to stay on my own for a couple of hours, then I became a 'latch key kid!'

Mrs Jacob at number 37, was quite elderly, and her family felt that she was becoming too frail to live alone. When I was ten years old she moved out to live with her daughter's family. She told my mother that a relative of hers was to take the house and she was also named Jacobs. However she was not quite what any of us quite expected.

On the day that Lilly and Tom moved in, we were curious. Would I call her Auntie Lilly or Mrs Jacobs? I didn't know yet. On first meeting her properly, my mother addressed her as Mrs Jacobs, and she corrected her quickly. She said that Tom was her second husband and that he was Polish, so her name was Nowika, pronounced Novitska. But she asked if everyone would just call her Lilly. Old Tom as we all referred to him, had a strong Polish accent, and he was very much a 'handy man'. He built a lobby onto their front door, and Lilly showed my mother the bathroom and kitchen cabinets he had built. Everybody admired his work. But Lilly seemed to think that it was Tom that they admired. My mother had him build cabinets in our bathroom and a front porch, and Lilly hung around most of the time with the excuse that she was helping him. People soon realised that she was also quite nosey, and wormed her way into all the families.

Kevin told me that they were getting cupboards from Lilly and when I told my mother at dinner, she looked at my father and said, "Bloody woman, she gets everywhere!" But she didn't become one of the women's kitchen group. They preferred to talk about her rather than to her. She was the new focus of gossip. "She hung around and watched him constantly when he built my cupboards!" my mother told the others. "She thinks that every woman is after him, HIM!! An old man like that!" Auntie Phoebe raised her eyebrows, "Some say she's not really married to him even." This was regarded as a terrible scandal in their society. "She can't even pronounce his name properly so I wouldn't be surprised," my mother added.

Lilly had a daughter named Sally, and Sally had a daughter named Susan. I liked it when they came to visit because I played with Susan. Sally was another subject for gossip because she wasn't married either. She was a tall, hard looking woman with a cross sounding tone in her voice. She had blond hair which was always neatly swept up into a top knot. She was always immaculately dressed usually in suits, but when she smiled it always looked as though she was doing it reluctantly. Her face did not smile with her thin lips, it remained stiff and tort. Her face was slightly tanned and she wore light pink lipstick.

Susan on the other had was a pretty girl with short dark curly hair. Uncle Mike said that she looked half Spanish like him. She laughed and smiled a lot. If they stayed for a few days, which they often did, Susan was allowed to sleep over in my house sometimes.

One day another family arrived to stay with Lilly and Tom. This was Lilly's other daughter Betty who lived in France. Her husband was French and they had a daughter Martine. I was fascinated by Martine. She had long brown hair which fell in ringlets around her face and her shoulders. I loved the way she spoke, and she said Ooh la la quite a lot. Betty was a stocky woman with tousled long dark hair and she looked a little unkempt. She seemed to be the exact opposite to Sally.

I wanted to play with Martine. She was my new best friend, this girl who I could hardly communicate with verbally. One day when I called for her, Sally opened the door and she automatically called Susan. But I said that I had come to see if Martine could play. Susan looked disappointed and Martine came out and happily skipped past the two of them and up the path. Sally became stiffer and crosser looking than ever. She scowled at me and her eyes narrowed and she pointed to Susan. "So what is she then, a bit of dirt?" I ran off down the path to join Martine.

Deep down, I knew that I was wrong and that Sally had every reason to be angry. However nothing more was said and Susan forgave me and we played together again.

That night, a tragedy occurred in our street. Auntie Mary had opened her front door and had become distracted by something in the house for a moment. Sheba had got out and ran into the road, into the path of a car. Ours was not a busy street traffic wise, so Sheba was very unlucky. The family were devastated to lose her like that so suddenly and unexpectedly.

About a week later my father arrived home from work. It was Wednesday and my mother at that time only worked on Thursdays and Fridays, so she was at home. He never took his car to work, because it was too difficult to park in the City of London. He came into the house very angrily because at some time that day our car had been scratched. We all trooped out to look at the damage. There was a long deep groove along the side of the car. My father said it had been done with a coin, or with keys. Then we were joined by others who had similar damage to their cars, including Martine's father's French car. There were lots of comments about who may have done this: Kids, teenagers, hooligans, mods, rockers, beatniks or communists!!!! But nobody had seen it happen. But the following night, all hell let loose in our street!

I was upstairs in my bedroom which overlooked the street. I liked my view. I could see our street, the flats across the road, the main road, the university which had Harry Neal's Moon on the top, which had been there for about three years or more. Lizzy could only see back gardens and the alley way from her room. In the old house, we shared a room but I liked that view because I could see into Sharon's garden. This evening I was getting ready for bed. It was getting dark outside so it was quite late and quiet because all the children had gone indoors. But the quite was disturbed by a sudden burst of loud shouting on the street.

It was adult voices, and the shouting persisted, so I had to have a peep. I ran to the window and kept behind the net curtains so that I couldn't be seen. Outside Lilly's house there was Auntie Mary, Ruth, Lilly herself and Betty her daughter.

"Don't you dare accuse my dad!" yelled Ruth, "I saw him looking at all the cars on the day it happened," said Lilly. "That still doesn't mean it was him, get some facts before you go opening your big mouth and spreading lies!" Ruth reposted. Then Betty joined in and said, "Shut up you bloody Jew!" Now Ruth was really angry and she shook her fist yelling, "Don't you call me a bloody Jew you French bitch!" Tom appeared at the end of the path, pleading with his wife and her daughter to come inside. My mother appeared and asked Auntie Mary and Ruth to come in for a cup of tea to calm them down.

I sat at the top of the stairs eager to listen to their conversation. "I've tried to get on with her, I really have. When she had that bronchitis, I made her a pot of my Kreplach soup, but do you know what she did? She said it tasted disgusting and she couldn't eat it. I told her that she was an ungrateful mare. Now she's saying that Isaac scratched the cars."

So Mary and Lilly had fallen out over soup.

The next event after they left, was that Albert called in to ask what the commotion was about. My father related the whole affair to him, and he said that there had been a rumour going round that Isaac had done it because a car ran over his dog. My father dismissed the idea saying that Isaac was his long term friend and wouldn't have scratched his car, any more than Albert would have. They agreed that it was unlikely and Albert went home. A few minutes later, Auntie Sheila was at the door, hysterically accusing my father of saying that Albert scratched the cars!

My father found the whole episode totally amusing, but my mother was very angry and upset. I think that I have inherited my father's sense of humour. The more bizarre and ridiculous something is, the more it amuses me.

The following day Betty's husband and Martine went back to France, as it was September and school would be starting again soon. Betty stayed on for a while longer.

Days came and went. School started again, and life went on as usual. Betty seemed to suddenly disappear and we assumed that she had gone back to join her family. My mother casually asked if Betty had gone home, and Lilly told her that she had thrown her out for exposing her breasts to old Tom!! We felt sorry for Tom having to live with Lilly but he did back up her story. My mother asked him one day when he was gardening in the back, if Lilly had heard from the family in France and he replied in his wonderful demonstrative way, "Betty, my wife daughter, she show big breast," and he did the action with his hands demonstrating enormous breasts on his chest!"

The trees turned to colours of red, rust, and yellow, and slowly fell to the ground creating a colourful crunchy carpet on the pavements and grass. Then the cold set in and the bare trees made a lacy pattern against the grey skies and the damp air chilled us through and through. Christmas came, and we had an exciting time with Uncle Ben and Aunt Glad coming with all my cousins. On the night of Christmas, we all went to a party at Auntie Ethel's, and all the other cousins were there. After the festival season had finished, the drizzle and the fog made me feel quite miserable. I still find that time of the year bleak and depressing. Lilly became sick with another dose of bronchitis and died. I couldn't help thinking that if she had eaten Mary's soup she may have survived, but that's just part of my sense of humour!

Old Tom was heartbroken. Every time he spoke of her afterwards, he cried. Tom continued living in the house for some years. As he got older, neighbours helped him out with household chores and errands. 'Meals on Wheels', delivered a hot meal to him every day. One day he brought in a letter which he had received from Social Services. He wasn't very literate in English and he asked my parents to read it for him. It was a letter informing him that his Polish family were living in the Soviet Union, and were trying to find him.

We didn't know much about Tom's history and Lilly certainly didn't encourage him to talk about it and tell people anything.

He had become separated from his family during the war and was unable to locate his wife and daughter after the war had ended. He feared they had been killed as many Polish people had, and he migrated to England as others had done. Many families were lost to each other during those terrible times. He had never married Lilly, in case his Polish wife had survived. It was his daughter Maria, who was trying to contact him, and she was living in Moscow with her husband and two children. It was obvious from the letter, that there had been previous correspondence and my parents suspected that Lilly had destroyed it before he had a chance to see it. Sadly, his first wife had died a few year ago, but not during the war.

The following summer, Maria and her family came to England and visited Tom, and he was reunited with his own, long lost kin.

The Ginger People

He was quite something I thought. His complexion pale with a sculptured look about his face, as if some great artist had carved those sharp, near perfect features. But the eyes were most extraordinary; eggshell blue and unusually large, giving the feeling that you could drown in them. We called hair of that colour, strawberry blond and his was soft and fell around his shoulders like silk trestles.

So Will was a strawberry blond, as was his mother, father and his sisters. He towered over me as we danced to David Bowie's 'Sorrow'. I felt as if I was melting into him and melting away. Him and me!!! Now that would be a strange reality given that we were true childhood enemies.

He was younger that me by about two years, probably too young given that girls tended to mature earlier. I was nineteen, he seventeen, immature obviously. He looked at me frequently at the party, It was Kevin's eighteenth. I suppose I looked at him, I must have done to know that he was looking at me. Kevin worked for a company that had a branch in West Midlands, and he had invited several of his business telephone colleagues to the party as well. Dancing was finished and everyone was slouched on chairs or floor listening to Jasper Carrot's rendition of, 'Magic Roundabout' and falling about at lines such as 'I wonder if Florence is a virgin'. It looked as if the boys were in for an all-nighter! When I announced that I was leaving. Will jumped up from his position seated on the floor, and grabbed his jacket. I could probably have managed to walk past the other eight houses to mine in safety, but said nothing.

Outside my house, all I could think of saying was, "I hated you when we were kids!" He was amused, I could tell by his raised eyebrows and slightly upturned corners of his mouth. He said nothing. The eyes were on me like deep whirlpools. I had that strange sinking, melting feeling again and then was consumed in the warmth of kiss and kiss deeper and deeper. But still I couldn't help myself from pressing the destruct button, hanging onto that part of me that wouldn't lose control. This was my lifelong rival after all. So I quickly reverted to becoming dismissive and making glib comments.

"I have to go now, but if you are in the pub tomorrow, I might say hi!"

Well it worked, and with a blink back to reality, he stepped away. At once I regretted it but the damage was done, and no going back.

I think he decided at that point, even if he had liked me, there wouldn't be a, 'him and me', and I had no way of knowing whether or not there might have been. So ego probably bruised, he left.

He was in the pub next day, and didn't speak to me, but one of the Midland's boys asked me if I had said hi to him yet. Now it was my turn for bruised ego.

The ginger people did not live in our street, they lived in an adjoining street at the end where the shops were. If you right you came to the shops but left, were more cottages like ours. That was where they lived. The house was pretentions to say the least. They had a bay window built in with rippled effect in each pane, and white columns at each side of the door. I suppose the effect was supposed to be like the old houses that Georgina Clark lived in across the main road. But it looked odd we thought, different to the rest of the cottages.

Sharon and I and sometimes Kevin, would ride our bikes to the end of our street, left and past their houses, then back through Rita Brown's square and through the network of alleyways to our street again. We rode fast like duelling dragons hoping that ginger Will and Wendy Wallace were playing out. If they were, they would scream and chase us. "Don't come round here, go back to your street." We loved the sport, and did it all the more of course.

The Wallace family were a close knit family, well known

and liked in the neighbourhood. Terry was the dad, Sarah the mum, and the kids were: Wilhelmina, Wendy, William and Winnifred, the toddler. Wilhelmina was a teenager. They all had flaming red hair, and for the girls their locks cascaded down their backs like Virginia creeper in autumn. I think I feared Wendy the most. Her scowl looked purposeful and her eyes fierce. One day she almost caught up with me and she spit, sending projectile saliva hurling through the air. But I was just out of reach and the deluge missed.

My father drank in the same pub as Terry Wallace. It was a corner house on the main road, near to Uncle Solomon's butcher shop and Maria's café. It was an old building with glass chandeliers, whose crystals had lost lustre with age and grime, and red flocked wall paper on white background was now brown with years of tobacco staining. The Landlady was called Nancy, she had brassy blond hair. She was a loud brash woman with a high pitched screechy voice. My father used to refer to her as, 'Aunt Shouty!' The clientele were always the same, my father and his friends on Tuesday evenings and Sunday lunchtimes, and Terry and our Polish neighbour Tom, most nights.

Terry liked to boast! My father said that he was a, 'story topper!' He boasted about his house: his dimple glazed windows, his up to date appliances, and his wife who always had a holiday in Spain each year with her girlfriends, Nancy the landlady being one of them! As married women rarely holidayed without their families at that time, Terry was a, 'new man!' His wife was a liberated woman, allowed to travel abroad without him!

Sometimes his brother Charlie joined him in the pub. He was different to Terry, a younger man, tall with dark brown hair and bushy eyebrows. He was loud and opinionated.

"No good will come of your missus gallivanting around the world," he said one night sitting at the bar, "You mark my words, one time she just might not come back. She'll take off with one of those Latins, and you'll find her working in some bar on Torremolinos Beach! And it's no example to your Wilhelmina. Young girls need keeping under wraps these days, or they end up in all sorts of trouble."

My father found all this quite amusing. Charlie Wallace had neither wife nor children.

"What a pair they are", he said when relaying the conversation to my mother at home. "One likes to tell stories, and one likes to give advice for things he doesn't know about!"

Wilhelmina was a rare beauty. Her auburn hair was streaked with silvery blond and was styled in a fashionable beehive bun, pinned at the back and slick around the front and sides. Her forehead was covered by an evenly cut fringe. She was always heavily made up, with thick mascaraed lashes and pale pink lipstick. She looked as good in slacks and sweaters, as she did in printed summer dresses, gathered at the waist band and flouncing around her knees. She went to work on the underground like Mimi did. I saw her one day at the Lido, with another girl. They didn't swim though, they laid towels out on the grass, and basked in the sun, bodies shimmering with oil as they tanned themselves.

I sometimes saw Wilhelmina in Arthur's buying cigarettes. I never saw her with a boy. I saw her with her uncle Charlie quite a lot. Often, when I was with Lizzy, visiting Maria in the cafe, I saw them both come out of the station together. One day I saw them in the park, with Winifred who was happily swinging, sliding, climbing and whizzing around on the roundabout.

One day, Sharon, Kevin and I rode our bikes to their row of houses, hoping that Will and Wendy would come out and chase us. As we giggled in anticipation, the door opened. We thought ourselves in luck and got ready to speed off. But it was Charlie and he was shouting and gesticulating back into the house. I thought that perhaps Will and Wendy had seen us and were nagging to be allowed out, and had made him cross. Then He slammed the door so hard that the glass rattled, and he began stomping down the path. Then Wilhelmina flung the door open and was pleading with him to come back and talk. I remembered about what my father had said that night and wondered if she had got into all sorts of trouble like he had warned Terry in the pub.

We continued from time to time, to menace Will and Wendy on our bikes. Then we outgrew such antics and I only saw them occasionally in passing.

When I was eleven years old, my father came home after his usual meet up in the pub, and asked my mother if Lizzy ever went in to local pubs when she was on holiday from college. She didn't think so adding that her boyfriend Mike was too mean to take her anywhere that involved spending money. My father then said that Terry Wallace's oldest girl had been shot dead outside the Old Ship pub, near the Old Road, at the weekend. When the local paper arrived, it was front page headlines. My mother's comment was that these young girls don't know how to behave, and this is what happens. I had little idea of what she meant, and wondered how bad her behaviour must have been to get shot. My mother was very good at being self-righteous, and was always quick to judge. Prayers were said for the family the following Sunday, at church. I was quite traumatized by the whole event, and scared to walk past the Ship for ages after, in case somebody thought that I was badly behaved.

Then further news broke. She had been shot by her uncle, Charles Wallace, and he had been arrested. People had plenty to say, such as the fact that things had been carrying on for some years. I didn't know what they meant, and what had been carrying on.

Terry Wallace still frequented the pub, but my father said that he had changed. He sat at the bar with Polish Tom, and was very quiet. Tom knew all about loss, as his wife had died quite recently. I rarely saw the other members of the family, until Kevin's party, and my brief encounter with Will.

A year after the party, I made friends with Wendy, who was working in Education as I was. We occasionally socialised after work in local pubs. I never mentioned Wilhelmina and neither did she. I felt that it would have been too painful a subject coming from somebody who wasn't a close friend. Will joined us for a drink one night. That was awkward. I had never told Wendy about the party, but I think she sensed slight tension between us. I noticed her glance from him to me enquiringly, a few times. Even then, I regretted my behaviour that night.

The Other Half and how they Lived!

By the other half, I am referring to those who were probably termed as 'upper middle class', those more affluent people who lived in large houses in rich areas. I had experience of such people from quite an early age. My father worked for a printing company and managed an associated stationary shop in Bishopsgate, in the heart of the city of London. Employees ran the shop, whilst he ran the offices, and represented the company to local merchant bankers, stockbrokers and other city firms. He frequently took luncheon with clients and some, became more intimate friends which involved family visits out of office hours.

The Trent family lived in the 'stockbroker belt' in Purley, Surrey. They had a large house in a long road of huge properties. We were invited for Sunday tea, several times a year. I think that it was because of my father's involvement with such company, that my parents insisted that I spoke well, and didn't drop my letters T or H, or substitute TH for F or slur my vowel sounds. At school the other children called it 'talking posh', and I tended to revert to my Cockney accent in the playgrounds, but I think that I never quite pulled it off. I was still posh!

I liked visiting the Trents, and I loved the big house. There was a gravel driveway leading to the house and they of course owned a Rolls Royce. On entering the house, there was a very large entrance hall, and at the back of the hall were sweeping curved staircases at each side leading to a landing which overlooked the hall. At the back of the landing were the doors to six bedrooms and two bathrooms. The downstairs rooms consisted of: a large kitchen and pantry, a dining room which doubled as a games room, a music room, a cloakroom, and finally an enormous lounge which they called the parlour, and it had an inglenook fireplace and a grand piano in the corner. The garden was extensive, my mother referred to it as Trent

Park. It was beautifully landscaped and of course maintained by a gardener.

Mr Trent, or William as my parents called him, was a lovely man. My parents respected him very much, but my mother did not like Pamela Trent, or Mrs Trent as I called her. She described her as a cold and judgemental woman, but she was always nice to me. There were four children. Edward was the oldest and he was my sister Ann's age. My mother said that he was a delightful boy. Annabel was next, and she was a nurse. I was in awe of her. She was very pretty with fair curly hair. She played the piano and spent much of her time in the music room. James came next, and my mother said that he was obviously Pamela's favourite child and she showed her favouritism in front of the other children. Richard was the youngest. He was four years older than me but he still enjoyed taring around the garden and playing with me, and with Lizzy until she got too old for that sort of thing. Hide and Seek was great there because there were so many places to conceal yourself.

We played all afternoon and the adults drank tea in the parlour and talked. Edward was often out, and Annabel would play her scales or play a sonata in the music room. At five o'clock precisely, we would all be seated around the enormous rectangular table with starched white table cloth and matching napkins. Tea was always salad and cold cuts, followed by cakes and pastries. They were prepared in the morning by the housekeeper, but she had Sunday afternoons off, so Pamela would carry the dishes through from the pantry.

Apart from the offer of various foods, it was an almost silent affair, as if the family had taken a vow of silence. Lizzy and I found it very strange, as we were very chatty at the table at home. After we had eaten, the table was cleared and the chairs moved against the oak panelled walls in the room. All of us helped with this, then finally the most amazing transformation would take place. The top the table was lifted off to reveal a full sized Billiards

74

table. The drinks cabinet would be opened and the ladies would take sherry and the men whisky. Often, I would watch for a while. I was fascinated by the dark green felt table and the shiny red and white balls which they hit with long sticks into little nets hanging from the corners and sides of the table. On the wall was a black and gold gilt board with numbers on it and a knob which they would slide along after each turn. This was the score board. I didn't understand the game at all. Sometimes they played a game with lots of shiny coloured balls called snooker.

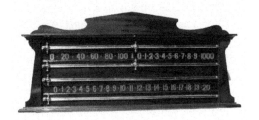

After tea, we were allowed in the parlour and left to amuse ourselves. Richard always took advantage of the absence of adults, and would proceed to say as many rude words as he could think of. I would roll about in fits of giggles at the fact that posh kids could be ruder than Stepney kids!

When I was six years old, we were invited to stay at the Trents for Christmas. We left home on Christmas Eve, and drove to Purley to stay for three nights. We walked into the hall, and there, at the back between the two staircases, stood the tallest Christmas tree I had ever seen. It reached almost to the ceiling, which was of course two floors high. It was covered with coloured lanterns which flashed on and off. It was magical. I stood and stared at it, almost afraid to blink in case it disappeared. That night, Annabel played carols on the grand piano in the parlour, and we sang along. I knew the words to: Jingle bells, we wish you a merry Christmas and away in a manger, so I joined in with those.

The next morning, Annabel took me into the music room, where there was a pile of wrapped presents which she said were for me. I had opened my presents at home before we left, and now I had more. Mr and Mrs Trent had given me a bobble hat and matching mittens. They were pink and fluffy. They also gave me a doll, but Annabel gave me the best present of all, it was a nurse's outfit complete with a mask, a watch, a thermometer and a stethoscope. Lizzy had presents too, but they were boring grown up things like a pen and a diary.

Christmas dinner was much livelier than the usual silence at Sunday tea. My favourite part was finding a shiny silver sixpence in the pudding which I was allowed to keep. I shared a room with Lizzy during our stay, and it overlooked the garden. It snowed on Christmas night and it made the garden look like a scene from the Ice Queen. Mr Trent had put nuts out on the bird table which brought squirrels and birds scurrying to the feast. We didn't see scenes like this in Stepney. I had never seen squirrels in a garden before, not even at Uncle Ben's house in Hertford.

The day after Boxing Day we went home. It had been a magical Christmas and I couldn't wait to play nurses and doctors with Sharon and Kevin, wearing a real uniform with a stethoscope and thermometer.

We continued our trips to Purley throughout the next few years. As Kenneth grew older, he became even worse, telling smutty jokes and using rude words and singing rude songs. He took to calling my sister Lizzy Dripping, which did not please her very much.

When I was nine years old, my father came home from work with some terrible news. Edward Trent had died. My mother was shocked and upset because she really liked Edward. She didn't speak for some time, then asked my father what had happened. "He was in his London flat, and he had blocked all the door areas so that air couldn't get through, and he turned on the gas."

My mother began to cry. "It's all her fault you know." She said angrily through her tears. "She always treated him as if he was a disappointment, and then she turned him out when she found out that he was, you know!!"

My father then continued to say, "According to William, the boyfriend he was with, left him."

"What do people do at a time like that?" my mother said, "They turn to their family, but she made that impossible didn't she. I stand by what I said, it's Pamela's fault."

I understood that Edward had died, but not much else. "Oh by the way," my father said, "He also told me that Annabel is going to be married. It's only a small affair, just close family."

Annabel married a man named Miles. I thought it was a strange name. Nobody I knew was called Miles. William gave my mother a wedding photo after the event had taken place. I didn't think she looked like a bride at all! She wore a beige suit and a brown fur hat, well that wasn't anything like a bride's dress. Miles had hair at the sides but in the middle he was bald. My father had that, but he was very old and Miles looked old as well. Annabel was much too pretty for him. A few months later William told my father that Miles had turned out to be a disappointing husband. He was always out at his golf club and Annabel was left at home by herself. She was also going to have a child.

When I was eleven years old, Lizzy went away to college and didn't come to visit the Trent's anymore. One Sunday, when we were there, Richard had invited his friends over in the evening. He was fifteen. The adults were having their usual session in the Billiards room, and we were all in the parlour. Richard got out his tape recorder and pulled a reel of tape out of a box. He had lots of pop tapes recorded from the wireless and television, but this one was marked Rugby. I assumed it would be a boring sports tape, my father sometimes listened to football or rugby on the wireless. Richard set up his tape, and the boys gathered round. I was poised for boredom, but when he turned the machine to play, it was singing. The first song was, 'Dinah show us your legs, a yard above your knees!' The boys were singing along with the very vulgar words and falling about laughing. That was my introduction to rugby songs and I thought they were hilarious. It was also the first time I met Melanie.

Richard was poised to snap the tape recorder to stop and watched the door carefully. He reacted at the first turn of the door handle, and stopped the songs. It was in fact James with his girlfriend Melanie, returning form a cricket match. She was the most beautiful girl I had ever seen. She had long honey blond hair. Her eyes were bright and blue and they smiled. Her skin was smooth and her complexion perfect without any makeup. She was a true beauty. Everybody loved Melanie apart from Pamela, who reluctantly accepted her, because nobody was really good enough for her precious James, or so my mother said.

When they married, it was a huge affair. We were all invited. She looked like a fairy tale princess in her white satin and lace gown and net veil cascading from a crystal tiara. Her hair fell in ringlets toughing her shoulders at each side in front of the veil. She carried a posy of yellow and white freesias and the scent was heavenly. I imagined myself looking like that, but knew that I would never be that beautiful.

Richard met his future wife when he was just eighteen. I was a teenager by then. June, as she was called, didn't look like June at all. June is a sunny, carefree name for a fun-loving, carefree girl. She didn't have a sunny disposition, she looked quite scary. She was very business-like and I thought cross looking. She had brown shiny hair cut into a bob. Her face was pale, and the cut of her hair embraced her sharp angular features. Nobody apart from Richard liked June, and she didn't warm to the Trent family nor they to her. I didn't go to the wedding as I was away for the weekend singing with the choir I belonged to.

My mother's report of events were less than complimentary. June ignored Pamela and Melanie was in tears because June had ignored her new-born baby. My mother blamed Pamela as always saying that she had driven Richard out and he had married somebody he was not suited to. Even I wondered why the fun loving boy I always knew, chose such a serious wife! Reports on how the couple fared, from my father via William, were not favourable either. June was often in Europe on business and she didn't want children. She had very little to do with the family, and when Richard visited, it was always on his own. Apparently they had asked him why she never came and he had said that it was because she felt strange. My mother added that what she really meant was that she felt strange amongst strangers.

After the children had left the family home, the Trents decided to downsize and they moved to a smaller house in the area. I only visited once, because I hated the new house. I think that I felt that way because I had loved the old house so much. My parents continued to visit occasionally.

One day my father came home with news that James had left Melanie and had moved in with Richard and June.

He also said that William had praised June for how kind she had been during this difficult time. My father questioned the event because Melanie was supposed to have been the family sweetheart!! But apparently she was having an affair with the milkman. I had to laugh secretly to think that people of that so called upper middle class, still did such things as have affairs with milkmen!!

By the time William died, all the siblings were estranged from their spouses. If it taught me anything, it was that you cannot buy a happy life! There was no shortage of money, but not one of them was truly happy. The constraint of appearance and being judged if anything happened that didn't fit into their society, had taken its toll on all of them. My parents lost touch with the family after William's death, although some of William's city colleagues told my father that Pamela remarried.

Markets and Walking to Bow and Beyond

Markets were a treat because when we were going to the market, there was a good chance I would be coming home with something good. It could be a toy, or something special and delicious to eat, or something new to wear. Some markets were small, and some seemed to go on forever.

The closest market was called the waste. It ran along the pavement by Whitechapel Station and was opposite the Royal London Hospital. It was a small market and there were: fruit and vegetable stalls, household goods and some clothing. I was allowed along the waste by myself when I was about nine years old. I couldn't work out why it was called the waste and Lizzy said that it was because it was in the middle of Stepney and Aldgate, and your waist was in the middle of your body so that was why it was called that. So now I knew!

There were other markets we went to, much bigger markets. Sometimes on Saturdays, Lizzy would take me to the 'Roman', which was a very long market stretching along Roman Road. It was very good for buying clothes but there was not much else there. But sometimes on Sundays after church, we would go to 'The Lane'. That was near Aldgate and it was enormous, stretching through several streets. That market had clothes, toys, food, flowers and even pets. The Lane was short for Petticoat Lane, but it didn't just sell petticoats, it sold everything. I loved all the stall holders shouting out to advertise what they were selling. There was one man who used to shout out, "Clothes for sale on the cheap, all knocked off!" I knew that it meant they were stolen, and wondered why he didn't get taken away by the police!

The Waste at Whitechapel.

Petticoat Lane.

Walking to the waste on my own was good. I would walk to the end of our street, past the shops like Arthur's and the chemist, then cross the road at the traffic lights, and turn into the main road. I had to pass the underground station and the Mooney swimming pool. Next I passed the brewery and the ABC cinema where I sometimes went to

Saturday morning pictures with Sharon and Kevin. Beyond this was a shop called a Supermarket where my mother used to like coming because she got Green Shield Stamps when she bought things. The pavement the widened and there were gardens at the pavement edge which you could walk through or have a rest on the park benches. When you passed the gardens you came to the waste.

I rarely bought anything, but I would walk along browsing at the stalls, then walk back looking in the shop windows at the back of the pavement. When I was a little older, I would often come here for the record shop Wally for Wirelesses, and buy my favourite hits.

But the Waste wasn't far and I decided that I wanted to walk further. To my mind, walking a long way seemed to signify being more grown up.

So I decided to walk to Bow. Walking to Bow was in the opposite direction to the Waste. I had to go to the main road, walk past the flats and the University. When I reached Mile End Station, I turned down a narrow but long road, which led into Bow Common Lane. I then walked along this road until I reached the Cemetery where I would turn back.

One day, I decided to walk through some flats and go into a small swing park, and have a go on the swings and the roundabout. There were other children in the park but I noticed a particular group of three girls, standing near the monkey poles, looking at me as I sat on a swing. They began to make their way over to the swings. A girl with long stringy untidy black hair came up to me and said, "What are you?" Not being sure what she meant, I answered, "A girl."

"Yes but what are you?"

Still puzzled, I replied, "I don't know what you mean."

"Are you a Cafflik or a Christian?"

Now I was really confused because my parents said that Catholics were Christians. Kaye and all her family were Catholics and Kaye's brother Brian was married to my sister Ann.

The girl continued, "If you're a Christian you can't play in the park, cause we're Caffliks, and Caffliks are better than Christians!"

Then I remembered a word that I think my mother said that we were, and I quickly blurted out, "I'm a Prodistone!"

"Never heard of it, what is it?"

I carried on, "My sister is married to a Catholic."

"Oh then you're a Cafflik cause Caffliks don't marry Christians, so you must be a Cafflik! You can play in the park!"

By this time I had lost the will to play anywhere and as they went back to their monkey poles, I quietly left and continued walking home.

About a year after this incident, my mother said that I was old enough to travel on a bus by myself, and not long after this I was allowed to go on the underground. I had several school friends who were also allowed to go on buses and trains, so we started going everywhere. We would go by bus to Victoria Park, or to the Whitechapel Art Gallery or the Bethnal Green Museum where all the doll's houses were. One day, when I was on my own, and it wasn't a working day for my mother, I made my way to Liverpool Street Station and walked to my father's office in London Wall, asking the way from a few passers-by. My father telephoned my mother and told her I was with him, and not to worry about me. He then took me to a restaurant in the city where he met Mr Trent, and bought me lunch.

I then started going to London Museums with my friends from school like ghostly Jackie and Koko from the big flats. We used to take our slippers and a notebook and pencil. We drew pictures of mummies in the British Museum and animals in the Natural History Museum. The entrance was free and our parents gave us money for the trains. On Saturdays, we would often go to the Tower of London, because that was free on Saturdays. My favourite place of all, was St Paul's Cathedral. We would climb the stairs to the Whispering Gallery, and go to different sides and talk to each other through the walls. I had no idea how it worked but thought it was great fun. Then you could climb higher and go onto an outside balcony and see a fantastic view of London. You could even go higher but you had to climb up ladders and the highest ladder was to the golden ball at the top where you had to hang onto the ladder and look out. It was 365 feet high.

I seemed to be given the freedom to travel around like this at a very early age, and looking back, I think that my mother was very brave to let me do it.

Church Days and Brownies

My mother had the idea that if we went to church we would be better children, so we were sent. At first it was Sunday school. An elderly lady would take us to a room at the front of the church and read us stories about God and Jesus. Then we would draw pictures of Jesus walking on the sea, or giving out loaves and fishes, or Jacob climbing a ladder or Joseph in a colourful coat. Sometimes we sang hymns, and I liked singing. There was a song about Michael Row in a boat and I knew that boy, he lived in the flats in our street, but I didn't know Julie from the song about hoping to follow Julie!! We also learnt the Lord's Prayer, which was, 'Our Father, Harold be thy name', and so I thought that God must be called Harold. Once we were ten, we were too old for Sunday school and we had to stay in church.

The church itself was quite magnificent in its architecture which was fifteenth century with later additions from Georgian and Victorian eras. Furthermore, the history of the site preceded the currant building as it had first hosted a place of worship from 952 A.D. The village of Stepney had grown around the church, its central point. There are remnants of these times still within the latter building, most notably a Rood Stone showing the crucifixion. This tenth century relic is displayed at the back of the altar, and is a most revered treasure both for the church and Stepney itself.

There were also leper squints on the left side of the altar which fascinated me, although I didn't ever get to sit in one, and somebody said that you could catch leprosy if you did crawl into one. I did however get several chances to visit the belfry which was at the top of a spiral staircase and was very high up. The bells were cast at the very famous Whitechapel Bell Foundry. There were ten bells and the largest was one of the heaviest in the country. The first time I went up I was only six years old. It was after Sunday school and I was very excited on the way up, but coming down was another story. As I looked at the uneven narrow stone steps going down and down, I imagined myself falling, going round and round until I hit the bottom. I cried and I froze, and the priest had to carry me down on his shoulders. It was a few years before I ventured up again, but second time around, I wondered what all the fuss had been about.

The bells sounded magnificent when they rang, which was on Sunday mornings of course, and Wednesday nights when the ringers practised, and finally on Saturdays for weddings.

The church services were very long. It was a High Church Anglican service and the mass was sung. I looked forward to the end so that I could run across the road to King Street, to Aunt Meg's and see my cousins. Sometimes I went to parish breakfast which was in the local school hall and I had cereal and orange squash.

As I became more familiar with all the prayers and chants and intersessions, and could say them by heart, I liked church more. I made sure that I looked around so that everyone could see that I knew all the words and didn't need a book. If pride was a deadly sin, then I suppose I was very guilty of it. I became quite frustrated that I couldn't take the bread and wine, and couldn't wait to be older and get confirmed.

Once a month there were church parade Sundays, and all associated groups such as: Boy Scouts, Girl Guides, cubs and Brownies carried their flags into the church and they were displayed at the altar during the service. I was a Brownie and I and all the others, wore our uniforms on these days. I felt proud because all the church congregation saw me in my uniform, notwithstanding the fact that the Brownies could see that I knew all the prayers and chants by heart.

I liked Brownies. A priest's wife from church was our Brown Owl, and I liked playing team games, having Pow Wow time in a circle, and doing tests. We got Brownie points for having a smart uniform and shiny badges. Brown owl said that we needed to polish our badges with elbow grease, so I asked my mother to buy some. She and my father laughed for days about this, and I couldn't understand why. But my mother got me some metal polish, and I had a lovely shiny badge. I was a Brownie for four years, and I became a group leader or Sixer as we were called. I passed all the tests, I was a very good Brownie.

The year I finished being a Brownie and became a Girl Guide, was the same year that the Rector in the church retired. I was very sad, as he had been the only Rector I had known. His replacement was a much younger man named Father Gilmour, and the good news was that he had three children, all girls, close to my age. I was quick to make friends with them and stopped visiting Aunt Megs so often after church. Instead I would go to Parish Breakfast which was now in the rectory, and we had hot dogs and not cereal. Mrs Gilmour made huge trays of them and they were very popular. They were delicious. Then I would play with the girls, often in the big garden if the weather was okay.

Church attendance increased that year as Father Gilmour did a lot to entice people to join. There were clubs, outings, fetes and parties.

When I was twelve, I was confirmed. It was a big affair. I had a new outfit, blue culottes and a matching waistcoat. This was very fashionable at the time. The Bishop came and put his hands on our heads, and we had to have a sponsor. I didn't really know the lady who sponsored me but she had obviously noticed me in church, and after this she and her husband became good friends with my parents. It was at this time that my parents made the decision to become church members themselves. It didn't take them long to build a circle of friends and join the parish council.

The youth club which was run by another of the priests became known as the Sunday Club as we met on Sunday evenings. The core members of the group stayed friends for many years and some of them even married each other eventually.

Church life was far from perfect, but I owed much of my social life through my teenage years, to the church. Although I lost touch with most of the people when I married and moved away, I still think of most of my peers from the church, and the elders, as people I felt comfortable and safe with.

I left Girl Guides shortly after moving up from Brownies. I didn't like the Guide leader and she made it quite clear that she didn't think much of me. She allowed a group of girls to bully me, and one evening after Guides, I was set upon by this same group of girls. I was badly bruised from being punched and kicked, clumps of my hair were pulled out. The Guide Leader said that I had deserved it because I talked about them and their parents. I wasn't sure to whom I was supposed to have done this talking, but she was happy to believe them. Clearly, this was not a place where I could feel safe!! I never went back.

Synagogue Days

My parents moved to Stepney after World War II. They took over the tenancy of a drapers shop with a flat above. My father returned to the company he had worked for previously, before he was conscripted to the army. This company was based in the City of London. My mother ran the shop. They became close friends with their Jewish neighbours, Joan and James. They were frequently in and out of each other's homes for cups of tea, or chats, or to borrow something. On Tuesday evenings, and Sunday lunchtimes, they went to the local pub just across the road to the shop. The aunts and uncles in our family would often join them, and Joan and James had brothers and sisters who also came along. There was also another man, a bachelor, who lived close by who regularly joined the merry party, and his name was Jack. He lived in some flats close to the local Grammar School.

By the time I was born, the shops and houses in that row were demolished for new flats to be built, and the families were rehoused. My family were rehoused to a cottage with a garden, which was my first place to live as a child. Joan and James moved further afield, but James sister Mary and her family were moved to our street. Another of the brothers Solomon lived close to my Auntie Ethel just across the road from our street. My father found a new local pub and continued the Tuesday and Sunday visits joined by Uncle Solomon and Jack, who would walk down from the old neighbourhood. They were my father's closest friends.

These were the people I grew up with and was very close to. They were all called Uncle and Aunt by me of course.

Uncle Solomon was a big man who seemed to always be smiling. I thought that he must be very happy all the time and obviously nothing bad ever happened to him to make him stop smiling. He was a butcher by trade, and his shop was in the main road opposite the station and the Mooney swimming pool. My mother would not buy meat from anywhere else. She was insistent that kosher meat was safer than any other because it was killed in a hygienic way and the meat was always in the shop within twenty four hours of slaughter, therefore it was fresh. My father was allergic to pork, so it was of little consequence that kosher butchers didn't sell it.

Going to uncle Solomon's was never a quick affair as he was such a friendly man and he could talk for England and Israel together. It could be worrying as he gestured with his hands as he talked, and more often than not, with his butchers knife in his right hand! I was glad to be on the other side of the counter. My mother always bought the same things: necks and scrags of lamb for stew, stewing steak for pies, porterhouse steak for frying, Chicken or a beef joint for Sunday, calves liver, and beef chipolatas in a long string which always made me think of Punch and Judy.

Sometimes I used to go to the shop by myself to pick up the order. I loved doing this because as a treat, Uncle would give me little slithers of raw steak which I found delicious. If my mother was there she wouldn't let me have it because in spite of the freshness, she still considered it dangerous to eat raw meat. I can attribute my love of rare meat dishes to Uncle Solomon. Some of the other ladies in the queue often remarked that I didn't look like a Yiddisher girl but I didn't tell them that I wasn't.

There was only one thing I disliked at the shop, and that was the back room. That was where Ivan, Uncle's son, and sometimes Auntie Mary, prepared the chickens. They would pull out the feathers, and burn off the tiny remaining ones with a blow torch. You could smell the singed flesh and stubble. They then cut off the head and feet. That wasn't too bad, but finally they would split the belly and the guts would come spilling out into a bowl which they had ready and they scraped out what was left, including unformed eggs. It made me feel sick, so as they

91

always kept the door to that room open, I made a point of not looking that way. It didn't put me off eating chicken though!!

When Auntie Mary used to look after me, between school ending and my parents getting home from work, I looked forward to Friday evenings. It was a very busy time in Auntie Mary's home. She would cook all the dishes and get the big candle stick out. It was called a Menorah and it held seven candles. My mother told me that each candle meant something different and it was very special. Auntie Mary said that they would all do special blessings called Kiddush and eat before the sun went down. Then the Sabbath would begin, and this was a day of rest when all the Jewish shops were closed. That was why we didn't buy any meat on Saturday.

I enjoyed special days at the Synagogue. It wasn't like church at all. The men sat downstairs and the women sat up in a gallery. The men wore little caps on their heads, and the women wore hats or scarves. They didn't have a priest, they had a Rabbi and he would come out and sing in another language which my mother told me was Hebrew. The women upstairs would start to chat, and after a while the men would look up with disapproval and you would hear schhh----. For a while the chatter would cease but would gradually resume and there would be another rebuke from below, and so it would continue until the end. Uncle Solomon used to call it shmoozing which meant gossiping.

Sometimes there would be a feast in the Shul if it was a special time, and all my favourite Jewish foods would be there to enjoy.

I learnt lots of Yiddish words. Sometimes my parents would drive up to a place called Stamford Hill and buy Vienna Sausages and chopped liver and fish, and salt beef for Sunday tea, and shtrudel which was a sweet pastry, for desert. I was fascinated by the men who wore long black coats, big hats, and had a long curl hanging down in front of each ear. I even saw little boys dressed like it. My parents said that they were a certain type of Jew. Auntie Golda and Uncle Solomon called them frum, which meant very religious. If they ever discussed anybody who they thought was strange or crazy, they called them Meshugener, which meant crazy. Clothes were often called shmatteh which really meant rags. I still use all these words.

As well as special Jewish holiday services, we went to Weddings, Funerals and Bar Mitzvah's, the latter being a celebration for boys when they were grown up which was thirteen. The weddings were the best. When Ruth got married, she looked beautiful. She had a white lace gown and veil. As usual, we were in the gallery, but nobody was shmoozing, every one watched and listened carefully. Ruth and her bridegroom stood under a sort of rectangular tent with open sides, and we could just about see them from upstairs. The Rabbi did singing and said many words which they responded to and then they were given some wine. They drank the wine and placed the empty glasses on the floor and stamped on them so they smashed. Then everyone shouted 'Mazel Tov' which meant good luck. I thought it was wonderful.

Every autumn, my parents went to what they called, 'The Jewish Do!' My mother would have her hair in a bun and often sprayed it gold, or wore a thin hairnet covered in pearls. She had a new evening dress every year and she always looked beautiful. Auntie Golda never went and often ended up looking after us. I couldn't wait until the next morning, because there was always a doll for me which they had won on the tombola along with other prizes. When I was sixteen, I was allowed to go, and it really was an amazing evening. I continued going until the year I married. That was also the year that Uncle Solomon died, and my parents never went again. I think that my father could not face going without his best friend being there.

The No Good Girl

The house that we exchanged with the Rust family, was an end of a terrace on the roadside rather than set back behind fenced grass squares. Auntie Mary lived three doors away, but next door to her lived a lady named Rosa. She was a lady of about my mother's age, and she had light brown curly hair. She wore a flowery pinafore, and never seemed to go out. She lived with her daughter Myra and Myra's two little sons Barry and John. They never played out with Sharon, Kevin and me.

One day, their door was open and they were playing on the doorstep with toy cars. I seized the opportunity and started talking to them.

"I'm waiting for Sharon to come out," I said. They both looked up at me and then carried on playing cars.

"When she comes, do you want to play with us?" I asked

"We're not allowed off the step," said Barry, the older of the two.

"Can I play with you then?" I asked.

Barry shrugged his shoulders and said, "Suppose so".

Fickle as I was, I forgot Sharon and started playing car races with my new found friends, on their doorstep. Then Rosa came out and told us to come into the kitchen for orange juice. Then we played in their garden for a while until I heard my mother calling me from our garden. I ran home quickly eager to talk about my new friends. My mother asked why I wasn't with Sharon, and I shrugged and said that she hadn't come out. I told her all about my afternoon with Barry and John my new friends but she just looked at me and said, "Well don't forget your old friends!"

I told Sharon about Barry and John, and a few days later, they were out on the step again so we went along and sat down on Rosa's step.

"Where's your mum?" I asked.

"At work, in the bank," answered John.

"What about your dad?" asked Sharon.

"Oh he lives in another country."

"My sister lives in another country, she lives in Canada," I said excitely.

The Barry joined in, "Our dad lives in Greece, we are half Greek."

"I'm half Spanish," said Sharon.

Not wanting to be left out I piped up, "I'm half Canadian!"

Sharon laughed and said, "No you're not. Just because your sister lives there it doesn't make you half Canadian! One of your parents has to be born there for that, like my dad was born in Spain and their dad was born in Greece."

Sharon was an authority on everything, but I thought I'd give it a try anyway. The conversation continued with Sharon enquiring, "So how comes your dad doesn't live with you?"

Barry answered her, "He's working in Greece, but he's coming to England soon and he's going to get us a big house, and we're gonna live in the countryside and have a great bit garden to play in. Not a little garden like Nanny Rosa's."

"My uncle Ben lives in the country with a big garden, and so does Mr Trent," I said.

We played car chasing and Rosa brought out some orange juice and biscuits for us. It was one of those barmy summer days and we played and talked and laughed, enjoying every moment of the sunshine and school holidays as it was. We sat on the doorstep with nobody bothering us. Through the flats, we could see the traffic of the main road, but we were in our safe haven.

It wasn't long before Barry's revelation came to pass. I knocked on Rosa's door one Saturday, and Myra answered. She called the boys and said they could play for a little while, but they were going out soon. The boys were very excited.

"Our dads here," said John, "He came last night, and

95

we're going to Victoria Park."

We played races in the back garden until a tall man with black wavy hair appeared at the back door.

"Can Ellen come to the park too?" asked Barry. The man said that he didn't see why not as long as my mum allowed it. He seemed to be a very kind man. My mother on the other hand was not so easy going about it. I was quite puzzled when she said, "I don't really like you playing with them." She thought for a moment then said, "Okay you can go just this once."

I ran back to share the good news, I was allowed to go. Myra was packing: crisps, lemonade, and a football for us to play with. Nikos their father was standing in the hallway holding each boys hand and he called to tell Myra that we would see her outside. I expected us to go to the bus stop, but to my surprise, Nikos had a car!

We all piled in the back, and Myra came out and sat in the front. On the way to the park, Myra and Nikos seemed to be arguing about something, until she told him not to carry on in front of the kids. We had a great time at the park. We played on the swings and slides and in the sand pit. Then we had our crisps and lemonade, and we ended up with a game of piggy in the middle with the ball. I was quite sensitive to the feelings of grownups, something my mother had unwontedly taught me, and I sensed some tension between my friend's parents on this afternoon.

When I arrived home, it was late afternoon and my mother was cooking supper. So I thought that I would ask why she didn't like me playing with the two boys. She looked at me in an awkward sort of way as if she was a bit reluctant to tell me. Then she began, "It's not the little boys I mind," she said, "But there is someone in that house who I don't like."

I couldn't imagine who she meant because they were all so friendly and kind. So I asked, "Who?"

"Rosa is a lovely lady," she continued, "And the boys are dear little boys, but Myra is not a good person. She used to be friends with Lizzy and Kaye, but then she started seeing boys and she was only sixteen when the older boy was born and she nearly had him adopted!"

"What does adopted mean?"

"It means she was going to give him away to a stranger. Then she and the Greek man ran away to Gretna Green in Scotland where people who are too young can get married without telling their parents. They had to go chasing after them and try to stop them, but they were too late. It nearly made Rosa ill and that's why I don't like her!"

I didn't see much of the boys after that, not because of my mother, but because school started again and they didn't go to my school. Then they did move away, like they said they would when their dad came to England. Rosa was then living in the house on her own.

It was a couple of years later that I heard mention of the family again. I was in the kitchen at Aunt Meg's and my older cousin Christine was there with her friend Tricia. They wanted to go out for a walk and said they would walk me home. So we slowly walked towards the Old Road then turned the corner, past the Rectory and down towards the shops. When we got to the corner of my street, Tricia said, "I know this street, this is where that girl who was no good lived." Christine said that it was then Tricia continued, "She went out with that gorgeous Tony from the flats, he's got a sports car now, and then she took up with a Greek bloke and had a baby!"

I knew they meant Myra. I also knew who Tony was. He lived in the small flats in our street, and his sports car was parked near our house. I didn't know that Myra had been his girlfriend though.

I didn't hear of Myra or the boys after this incident, until a couple of years later when I was in the chemist shop talking to Helen, a girl who Lizzy knew and who was now serving in shop. I was buying hair bands, and the door opened and Rosa came in. Helen greeted her warmly and asked after Myra and her family. She told Helen that she was going to stay with them at the weekend. She added that the boys were growing up fast and that Nikos had been promoted. He was an insurance underwriter she said and now Myra doesn't have to work. She said that Myra was thinking of opening a tea shop in the village though. So Helen asked to be remembered to her and the children. Rosa smiled and nodded, paid for her purchases and left.

Then Helen began to say how pleased she was that Myra and Nikos were doing so well, after their difficult start. She asked me if I knew the story, and I told her that I only knew that they ran away and married in Scotland, so she began to tell me more.

"Well Nikos was engaged to a girl in Greece, but his parents had arranged it and he wasn't happy about it. So one day, he just left and came to England. He stayed with friends he knew who ran a guest house in Bournemouth. Rosa and Frank were staying there with Myra on holiday. Nikos and Myra got to know each other and he told her that he would find a job and lodgings in London so that they could continue seeing each other. He did so and Myra got pregnant. Frank went crazy and said that she was never to see Nikos again. Frank and Rosa contacted an adoption agency so that the baby could be adopted after its birth. Nikos and Myra met in secret and planned to run away. Added to this, Rosa and Frank managed to find out where Nikos's family lived through the Bournemouth people, and they told them what had happened. So they also came to England, but by this time, the couple had gone."

"But I did hear that the parents followed them," I said.

"Yes, they guessed where they had gone, lots of young couples did it when the parents wouldn't consent to them marrying. But they were too late. Nikos and Myra married in the clothes they were standing up in and they had to tie string around their fingers for rings. Even when they got proper rings they still kept the strings. I am glad that Rosa has accepted Nikos because the year that all happened, Frank died of a heart attack, and I think that Rosa secretly blamed him for a while!"

I really liked this story and thought that people had been very unkind about Myra. But in those days, it was such a scandal to be pregnant if you weren't married, and it was always the woman who seemed to take the condemnation.

The Love of Water and Running with the Rough Kids

I used to go everyday both after school and at weekends. We were only allowed half an hour in the pool because the individual changing cubicles needed to be freed for the next customer. At first I only went in the shallow water, but I knew that soon I would be able to swim. I would teach myself, I just needed to practise. Then one day I did it. I guess it was, what is referred to as 'doggie paddle', but I had both feet off the ground and I was moving forwards. I arrived home brimming with excitement and pride, only to be disappointed that they were sceptical as to whether or not I was telling the truth. However several of my friends backed me up and they all soon accepted it and believed that I could swim.

I quickly progressed to being able to cross the width of the pool and back. My first venture into the deep end was a humiliating experience. I easily swam the length, but the lifeguard who was busily scrutinising my suspect style and badly formed strokes, sternly ordered me back into shallow waters. But as my strokes improved, I migrated to deeper waters without fear or needing to look convincing. I was a swimmer.

The deep end was usually occupied by older children and adults. There was a need to avoid jumpers and divers, but apart from that it was just relaxing. I loved to lie on my back, stretch out my arms and float. One you have complete confidence that you are buoyant, it is a wonderful experience. I loved the smell of the chlorinated water and the crystal clear blueness. This could only be experienced in the deep end as the shallow end was too full of splashing and noise to appreciate any of this. My mother said I was a water baby, the amount of time I spent at the pool. It was within easy walking distance of my house, through the flats, along the main road, across at the traffic lights near the underground station and past the

Chimney Sweep pub.

The building was quite grand looking from the outside. The marble white steps led up to the double doors, and a sign reading 'Municipal baths'. We all called it the Muni, or Mooney as I always wrote, when scribbling in my diary. Inside, there were stairs to the right, and a corridor straight ahead, leading to the pool.

One day when I was with some school friends, we felt like getting up to mischief, and we crept upstairs to see what was there. One door led to a balcony overlooking the pool, but the other larger doors were closed. We opened a narrow slit, and peeped through. To our surprise, there were rows of wooden cubicles each containing a white porcelain bath tub with huge brass taps at the end. We looked at each other aghast, I think it was the last thing we expected to find. Later, I told my mother about the baths upstairs and she said that they were for people who didn't have a bath at home. Aunt Meg didn't have a bath, but they used a large tin tub which they filled with hot water.

After looking upstairs that day, we ran down giggling and paid our sixpences at the kiosk, to enter the pool. The pool was twenty five yards in length. On either side of the pool were rows of tiny wooden cubicles where you got changed and left your clothes. Even though it was a bit tight, we would often double up so more people could get cubicles. Each one had a number, and when half an hour was up, the lifeguard called your number and your session was over. At the Kiosk outside, you could buy hot tea, and thick slices of toast dripping with butter. I only did this on Saturdays, because this was the only day when I wasn't arriving home at a meal time.

The deep end introduced me to new friends. There was a girl called Jessie, who was a very good swimmer and was training for the local championships. She could turn in the pool like those swimmers on the sports programmes on television. There were also some kids who I recognised from what my mother always called 'the rough flats'. It was through deep end swimming that I venture into new territories; making friends with the rough kids!

I liked Cathy Richie. She had short fair hair and was slightly freckled. She always seemed quite serious. Looking back, she rarely smiled or laughed, and was always very; matter of fact; about everything. She was always plainly dressed, and she never seemed to get up to any mischief, so I came to the conclusion that she wasn't at all rough. She always came swimming with her older brother Micky, and his friends. They were big boys of fourteen and we were only eleven.

One day, on the way home from Aunt Meg's, I walked through the rough flats, and became aware that someone was calling my name. Looking around, I caught sight of Cathy sitting on a doorstep.

"Is this where you live?" I asked, and she nodded. It was a ground floor flat, and the front door was open. I sat next to her.

"You weren't at the Mooney yesterday," she said.

"No I was visiting my cousins in the country"

"I've never been to the country, what's it like?"

"It's nice, we drive down some little winding roads with forest on both sides, and my uncle's house has a great big garden with flowers and trees and grass."

"Sounds lovely, but we haven't got a car so we couldn't go anyway."

"I'll ask my dad if you can come with us when we go again!"

Cathy nodded thoughtfully and said that she would like that.

Then a woman came to the door from inside the house. She looked like Cathy. She was wearing a pink headscarf which I could see was covering hair curlers. She had a pink candlewick dressing gown, and had white strapless sandals on her feet. She was smoking and although I could tell that she was younger than my mother, she had more lines on her face and her eyes were grey and sunken with puffiness underneath. She said nothing, looked out for a

102

few moments then disappeared back inside.

Now that I knew where Cathy lived, I called for her quite a bit. She introduced me to the other girls she played with, and we played runouts, and bulldog and had running races. We always seemed to be running about! Sharon said that they were all rough kids and that she would never go and play with them. But I loved going over there and running with the rough kids, who weren't really rough it seemed.

Cathy's house was a very busy place, full of teenage boys and girls, all friends of Michael and they seemed to come and go all the time. I recognised one of the boys as he lived near to Aunt Meg. I learnt that his name was Colin Jenkins and he often brought his sister Susan and his younger brother Stephen with him. The younger brother was about the same age as Cathy and me, but he didn't play with us or talk to us or anybody as it happened. I guess he was shy. Susan was known by everyone as Michael's girlfriend and she was a very reserved and also quiet, but I did see her in the street near Aunt Meg's one day and she stopped to talk to me. She told me that she wasn't Michael's girlfriend, and didn't really know why people said that she was. I liked her.

One night, I was looking out of the upstairs landing window at home, and a boy and girl walked into the alleyway beside my house. They stopped and began kissing and giggling. I should have gone away from the window, but I thought I recognised them, and curiosity got the better of me. My instincts were right, but the boy caught sight of me and began shouting at me, "Oye, stop spying! Go on fuck off!" It was Colin Jenkins with one of the girls I had seen in Cathy's house.

From that time onwards, some of Michael's friends became quite hostile to me whenever I called for Cathy. They would ask me if I had come to spy on them or even say to Michael, "What's she doing here?" I was beginning to feel quite uncomfortable. However, Cathy was still as friendly as ever so I didn't stop going there. One day when

I called, and nobody answered, then a voice called, "There's no one in." It was Michael sitting on the wall opposite the flats.

"I can't get in, that's why I'm here. They've been ages!" I went and sat next to him to wait.

"Can't you go to Susan's house and wait?" I asked.

"No, her mum and dad won't let me in their house."

"Why not?"

"Because I was in prison!"

"What for?"

"I raped a girl!"

I didn't know what that meant but I remember Sharon telling me once that Marilyn from Shelly Brown's square had been raped and it was something to do with ripping her clothes. I wondered why anyone would go to prison for ripping clothes, but thought that it didn't sound very serious.

"Oh," I said, shrugging my shoulders.

"Aren't you scared of me?" he asked.

"No not really! When will they be back?"

He stared at me with raised eyebrows and shook his head in disbelief. I think at that point he realised that I didn't know what it meant and that his ploy to shock had fallen on deaf ears. I decided at that point that I was bored with waiting, so I went home.

The next time I called for Cathy, a boy who they called Macker opened the door. He was a tall thin boy with very short hair. He looked at me with a smirk on his face and said, "I saw you on the wall with Michael the other day. Well Michael is going out with Susan so don't get any ideas!" I really didn't know why he had said any of this, but I did feel uncomfortable. I could hear other girls and boys laughing from inside the flat and saying that he had some cheek saying this to me, and then he added, "Cathy isn't here so piss off!"

I decided that after this incident, maybe they were a bit too rough for me, and I wouldn't go back. If Cathy wanted to play with me, she could come to my house, but she never did, and she didn't come to the country with me either. They also seemed to stop coming to the swimming pool so I didn't see Cathy there either.

A few weeks later, I was walking home from Aunt Meg's and I came face to face with Susan. I thought she might just ignore me, but she stopped and smiled.

"Hi," she said, "Are you walking up to the main road?"

"Yes," I answered, and she began walking with me.

"I heard that Macker was really rude to you," she said. "I hate him, he's a horrible boy and he thinks he's so clever. And I am not Michael's girlfriend. I don't even like him!"

I told her about what he had said to me about going to prison, and she laughed. "That's a complete lie! He is just trying to sound like a big hard man! I don't really like any of them. I only go with Colin to their house because we are both supposed to keep an eye on our little brother. So we all have to go. But Shirley, the mum, she makes me laugh, with her short skirts, and her supermarket shoes. You'd think she was a teenager, my mum wouldn't be seen dead dressed like that!"

"Where's their dad?" I enquired.

"Well he went away didn't he," she replied as if I should know the answer.

Then we came to the shops at the end of my street and went our separate ways.

That was the last I saw of her or any of the kids from the rough flats. I thought about the father having left, and felt quite sorry for Cathy and her family. My mother had never been happy about me going over there anyway. Then one day, my mother asked me the name of the girl I had played with and I told her it was Cathy Richie. She looked at my father and said, "I bet it's him! Did you ever see the father?"

"No," I answered, "I heard that he'd went away!"

"Oh he went away alright, away to prison! Was his name Kenny?"

I didn't know the answer to that question, but my

105

mother was sure that the man in the newspapers who had just been convicted of robbery and shooting a man dead, was their father. I must confess to feeling a little frightened, but at the same time a little excited that I really had been in the company of genuine rough kids!

Lizzy's Friends

My mother was always a believer in welcoming our friends into the home. I think that it was more a control thing, so that she could vet them and make sure they were suitable. Kaye Mack was always in our house and we were always in her house, and being sort of related; her brother being married to my sister Ann; no questions were asked. Kaye was a tiny girl and had long sandy hair which she wore in a ponytail or pigtails. Kaye and Lizzy often took me to the park, but Kaye was prone to mishaps. She fell off the swing and broke her teeth, and she fell off the monkey bars and broke her arm. She would always be in trouble at home, so she always came to our house, and it was left to my mother to smooth things over with hers.

The Mack's lived at the end of our alleyway and their house was on the corner of the money lender's square. Mr Mack died before I was born, and my mother said that he was a lovely man. The family were from Ballynahinch in Northern Ireland but Kaye was born in London. Ann's husband Brian was the oldest, then there was Tom who was very handsome and had been in the army. Teenage girls often hung around the alleyway or the square hoping to see him. My cousin Peggy went to the pictures with him once, and all the girls envied her. Then there was Pat, who loved dog racing and tennis, and then Kevin who loved football, and went around with a group of lads from the local area who also loved football. The oldest girl in the family was Mimi and Kaye was the youngest of all.

Ann and Brian lived in Canada. My parents had rented a shop at the end of our road which was to be Ann's Hairdressing Salon as she was a hairdresser. However when they decided to emigrate the plans were shelved and it became the chemist shop. I think that my mother blamed Brian for taking her away, and never quite forgave him. Brian had already been working in Toronto at a stockbroker's firm, and he was convinced that there was a better life for them in Canada. He already had a Canadian accent and when he was introduced to my mother's sisters they actually thought he was an American. My Aunt Nellie who swore all the time, took Ann aside and asked what she was doing with a fucking yank! But when they were married, Lizzy, Mimi and Kaye were all bridesmaids and so was Cousin Peggy. I was just a baby and too young to be a bridesmaid.

My parents often talked about Mr Mack, and how he died. Apparently he had gone to work and a policeman knocked at our door in the late afternoon. He told my father that Mr Mack had died of a heart attack at work and that he couldn't bring himself to deliver such dreadful news to the family and begged my father to do it instead. When my father broke the news to Mrs Mack, she just looked at him and said, "But I've cooked his dinner! Look it's all ready."

Mrs Mack was a character though, a formidable woman if ever there was. She was quite stout, with long brown hair, greying in places often tied and plaited, or in a bun. Her back door was always open and we could come and go as we wished. She always seemed to be cooking, and she was a great cook, her cakes and pies were amongst the best I have ever tasted. She was proud of her heritage and liked all things Irish. She liked pop music, particularly Merseyside groups, as many of them had Irish beginnings. She loved Spurs Football Team and often made her way to White hart Lane and stood on the terraces. Kevin always said that when he was there with his mates she always seemed to find them and stand near to them. Then they would nudge him and say, "Kevin yer mum's here," and he would hold his head in despair as she hollered abuse at the referee for booking Danny Blanchflower, her favourite player. She even invaded the pitch once when Spurs were playing West Ham.

Lizzy was a ballet dancer. She attended a very good ballet school in London, where many famous dancers had trained. She often did exercises at home and I would try and copy her. Sometimes she would dance to music and I would dance as well but not with correct steps like her. I used to like it best when she did Spanish dancing and I would put a net curtain on my head because Lizzy said they wore something called a mantilla on the head.

Lizzy had many friends. I was always in awe of them because they were big girls and did big girl things. I wanted to do big girl things, but I was never allowed. One day she and Janie from Sheila Brown's square came and collected me from nursery and when they got to our house, they cooked eggs and bacon. I wanted eggs and bacon but they said I was too young and would have to wait for dad to come home. So I cried.

Sometimes Lizzy and Kaye and Myra from our street, used to do dances and plays in the grass squares, and entertain all the neighbours. On Sundays, Lizzy didn't really have anyone to play with though because Kaye didn't come out on Sundays. Lizzy said that it was because Kaye was Holy on a Sunday.

Then Lizzy became friends with the two Lindas. They were tall girls. One had straight shoulder length hair and was very quiet. My mother said that she liked her but I think that it was more that she felt sorry for her, because her mum had died and she lived with her gran. The other Linda had short hair which she styled and lacquered and it always looked perfect. They were always talking about boys and they used to go into the garden and look at the boys who hung around in Kevin's garden with his older brother. There was Matthew who lived next door to Kevin, and Bryan who Lizzy liked. They were always in Kevin's garden because Bryan's mother was house-proud and didn't want them hanging around in her place. Kaye said they were just whipper snappers! I think she was used to her brother's friends, who were a bit older.

It was around this time that they started telling me not to tell the grown-ups about the things they did and said, or not to tell Sharon because she would tell. One day during the school holidays, on a Thursday when my mother was at work, Lizzy had lots of friends visiting. There were the Lindas, Janie, and Doreen from their school and a small pretty girl who I hadn't seen before. They were all smoking, even Lizzy, but I wasn't to tell anybody. My father smoked, so the smell of smoke wasn't really going to be noticed particularly. But they had to get rid of the dog ends because they had tipped cigarettes and my father smoked untipped ones. Later on they all started putting on makeup in front of the large mirror in the front room, above the mantelpiece. They looked lovely with blue eye shadow and pink lipstick. Linda with the nice hair was already wearing makeup, but she just put more on top of it. I never saw her once, not looking completely perfect.

When Lizzy was sixteen, she made friends with a Greek girl in her class named Maria. Her family owned a restaurant next door to Uncle Solomon's butchers shop. It was opposite the train station. Maria was beautiful with black silky hair and a slightly tanned complexion. She and Lizzy talked about boys a lot of the time, but Maria wasn't allowed to have boyfriends or go around with girls who had boyfriends. Lizzy told me that Maria would marry a Greek boy when she was old enough to get married.

Lizzy had her first proper boyfriend when she was seventeen, and then a different boyfriend when she was eighteen. Whenever she went out with a boy, if they walked past Maria's restaurant, they had to walk separately so that Maria's parents wouldn't see her with a boy. I remember almost getting her caught out once because I kept running between her and the boyfriend and laughing. They were very cross with me, and said that if I did it again, they wouldn't take me out.

Lizzy's first boyfriend was named Joe. He was Maltese. I didn't know what that meant so I asked Sharon and she didn't know either but said that it might mean that he ate lots of Malteasers. So I thought it must be that! I liked Joe. He always wore a leather jacket and he rode a scooter. It was the era of Mods and Rockers, and they were Mods. Lizzy had a suit made with a Beatle Collar. She and

Joe would go to the West End, on his scooter, to a club called the Bastille where lots of Mods went. One night Lizzy and some of her friends went to see Billy Fury who was her favourite singer. But I wasn't to tell my parents because they thought that she was just at her normal Ballet class.

I liked Joe because he used to talk to my goldfish and he made me laugh. He was nice looking and had black hair, combed back and greased which was in fashion at the time.

But Lizzy gave Joe up for Mike who was in her class at school. It all started when Lizzy had a party and all the boys and girls from her class came and Maria was happy because Dave who she liked came, even though she wasn't allowed to have a boyfriend. I didn't really see them because I had to go to bed. The next day, they all came round again to help with the clearing up. Then I saw Mike and Dave and I didn't think they were as nice looking as Joe. Then Mike started to visit a lot and he was Lizzy's new boyfriend.

I didn't like Mike because he was serious all the time, and he only liked classical music. He wasn't at all funny like Joe. Lizzy said that Joe wasn't so funny but just immature which she told me meant not very grown up. She said that Mike was much more intelligent, but I thought he was just miserable. I liked some classical music, but I liked pop as well. My father sometimes played Mozart, Tchaikovsky, Borodin and Strauss and I liked that and Lizzy's ballet music. But Mike liked Stravinsky and music that my mother called heavy stuff. I thought it sounded like a big noise with no tune. Mike used to refer to his own mother as an ignorant person, and I think that my mother suspected that he thought the same about her.

Lizzy was with Mike for a few years. She went to college in Eastbourne and he went to Brighton which wasn't far, so they could see each other often. Lizzy's first teaching job was in one of the Medway towns in Kent. She shared a house with two other teachers from her school. I

111

used to go there sometimes for weekends, as by this time I was well into my teenage years. It was very good fun going there and lots of other teachers used to come and visit. Lizzy saw less and less of Mike and then she stopped seeing him altogether. She had a new boyfriend now named Greg and he was the R.E. teacher at the school.

Greg's ambition was eventually to become a priest. I really liked him because he liked progressive pop music which had become my favourite genre at that time. A year later, he was accepted into Divinity College and he and Lizzy broke up. But I still used to visit him at his college and listen to all his records. When Lizzy was with Greg, she began attending church regularly and her church friends were fun as well. It was through church friends, that she met her future husband.

My 1966

I hate football. I like to watch tennis, formula one racing, cricket and athletics. My sister loves football. She is a Chelsea supporter, but watches any game whoever is playing. My father was an enthusiast and supported West Ham which was our local team. At one time, he used to go to Upton Park and watch home games, but being a frugal man, he decided at one point that it had become too expensive. From that time on, he stayed at home and watched his team play on television.

Some of his enthusiasm rubbed off on me. The first time in my life that West Ham won the F.A. cup, I was playing outside with Sharon and Kevin, but kept running inside every now and then to the progress. My parent's friend Jack was in the house to watch the game because he didn't have a television at home. I was very happy when at last I was told that West Ham had won the match.

The next day we were told that the whole team would come along the main road on an open top bus, displaying the trophy. So Lizzy and I walked through the flats, very excited, and stood on the pavement, opposite the university. There was nobody else there and I began to doubt, thinking that perhaps my parents had got it wrong. Then big Michael from the small flats further along our street, came and stood on the pavement near us. So I asked him what he was waiting for, and he looked at me as if I was mad, and said, "West Ham!" It was as if it was the stupidest question he had ever been asked. But I was totally reassured.

Soon after, my parents came and then many others, and the pavement began to get crowded on both sides of the road. It reminded me of the time when the Queen came along our road in her black car. There was a sea of bodies as far as the eye could see!

When they came, the bus moved very slowly and the cheering and waving reached fever pitch. Bobby Moore held up the silver cup decorated with claret and blue ribbons and was shouting through a megaphone, "Sing Bubbles, go on sing Bubbles". I remember thinking that he was the blondest haired man I had ever seen. My mother was exuberant for the remainder of the day. The event clearly lifted her spirits. We watched the news that evening, and saw the big bus arrive at East Ham Town Hall which was its destination. The whole area was packed with supporters, and we laughed when the camera zoomed in on a little blond boy crying because he couldn't see anything, and then being lifted onto the shoulders of the man he was with. I include this anecdote because I met the little boy in the crowd many years later, it was the person I married!

When I was ten years old, the world cup came to England. We went on holiday to Littlehampton that year, because my mother said that the beach there was beautiful, sandy and golden. Lizzy didn't come with us because she had gone to Europe with her boyfriend. We stayed in a guest house near the beach. We had two bedrooms, so I had my own room. My parent's room was very big, and had a lovely three piece suite and a television, as well as the bed.

We spent most of the day at the beach, but would come back to the hotel if there was a game and England were playing.

Littlehampton was a jewel; not over commercialised like Brighton with its amusements and Pavilion and huge hotels; and the sand was so soft and yellow, and the sea glistened in the sun making me blink if I gazed at it for too long. I played, I swam, and we picnicked and made our way back if there was an afternoon game.

The woman who owned the guest house was very tall, but a gentle, patient lady. She fostered three children and we often saw them playing happily in the conservatory or the garden. My mother remarked on how well behaved they were and how nicely they played.

We saw every England game in the knockouts. I was becoming a good candidate for an avid football fan. I knew the names of every England player. My favourites were of course: Bobby Moore, Martin Peters and Geoff Hurst, because they were from West Ham. I knew nothing about the strategies of the game, I thought that offside meant that the ball had been kicked off the pitch. All I knew, was that England were winning all of the games, and then they were in the final, playing West Germany.

We travelled home in our car, the day before the final because Auntie Ethel and Uncle Jim were having a party for their Silver Wedding Anniversary. They had hired a hall for the occasion. This was a great day. England were playing in the world cup final and then I was going to a party with all my cousins there.

My father didn't hold back enthusiasm when watching an important match. Every time England scored, he bellowed, "Goaaaal," at the top of his voice and I was sure that the whole street could hear him. At full time the score was two goals to each team and that meant that they had to play extra time. My mother gloomily said that this time we would not beat the Germans. I didn't understand that she was referring to the Second World War, I just thought she meant a different football match.

Believing my mother, that we wouldn't win the game, I decided that I would not watch extra time, but go and bath before the party. It was a decision that I regretted, as from the solitude of my bath tub, I heard my father's war cry Goaaal. As I soaked in my pink bubble bath which smelt of roses, I heard it again.

I missed the famous, 'They think it's all over' moment but was back downstairs for the numerous replays and the Queen presenting the golden cup to Bobby Moore. His hair looked white on the black and white television and matched the cup which also looked white. I think that the whole country were celebrating.

I wore my blue broderie anglaise bridesmaid dress from Mimi's wedding, which had been made into a short party dress. It still looked very pretty and I felt good.

All my cousins were there and we played outside the hall, came in for the food and later on everybody sang Bubbles and danced in a circle to:

We won the cup
Eee eye yippy oh
We won the cup!

Belgium

The first thing I ever ate in Belgium was whole tomatoes, stuffed with brown shrimp and seafood sauce. I still make this at home when I can get the shrimp. The first time I had Belgian chips, I couldn't quite put my finger on it, but they were definitely the best tasting chips I had ever eaten. My friend Nathalie tells me that it's to do with the grease they use! They all found me very odd asking for vinegar and they could only offer me white vinegar. They of course had mayonnaise or tartar, as I do now when I visit. I had never heard of an Ice Cream parlour, but Leuven had several, and they were my introduction to Dames Blanche, ice cream, whipped cream covered in hot chocolate sauce with a crisp sugar wafer.

My parents met Jack in the pub near the draper's shop they had after the Second World War. Jack was a bachelor and he lived with his elderly mother. His sister and her husband also came to the pub and they all became friends.

Jack had met Alicia when he was billeted with her parents whilst in the army. Jack was manager of a tea company and he began supplying my parents with tea at cost price. He spent his holidays in Belgium with Alicia and her family. She had married, and had a son Rudi. Sometimes Alicia would visit London and bring Rudi with her and they would stay with Jack and Mrs Warren, his mother. Rudi was my age and although we couldn't understand each other we still enjoyed playing together in Mrs Warren's flat. When I was very small and we were playing on her living room floor, the adults were chatting and Rudi was talking away to me in Flemish. At the end of each sentence, he looked at me and said, "Ja?" After a while I looked at him, and nodded, and decisively answered, "Ja!" The adults burst into laughter and clapped me.

When Lizzy was twelve years old, Jack took her to stay with Alicia for a week. She had a wonderful time, being taken to France, Germany, Luxembourg and Netherlands. All were in easy reach across the borders.

When I was twelve, Jack took me. He was to stay for two days and then return to England. Alicia was coming to England two weeks later and would bring me home. As young as I was, I was very fashion conscious, I had to have nice clothes and look the part. I wore a white trouser suit with flared trousers to travel, very up to date. We were to take the night ferry. My parents to us to Victoria Station to get the boat train to Dover Marine. Then it was all aboard the ferry to Ostend. Jack bought us supper in the restaurant and then we went into the Duty Free Shop to buy Christian Dior Perfume for Alicia, her favourite, and cigars for Paul. I bought sweets for Rudi. We then sat on the deck for a while until it became too cold and windy, then we went into the lounge and sat on comfy chairs.

Jack slept, but I was much too excited so I just watched people coming and going. A woman who was sitting near us began talking to me and asked if my father and I were on holiday. I explained that Jack wasn't my father, but a family friend who was taking me to stay with other family friends where I would remain for two weeks. So she told me a bit about Brussels and how beautiful it was.

The boat journey took five hours, and I savoured every moment of it. We both went up onto the deck to watch the boat cruise into the harbour at Ostend. It was dawn and first light was peeping through thin grey clouds. We had to wait for over an hour before the first train left for Leuven. It was the Brussels train, but we were to stay on until Leuven. I noticed that Belgium was a very flat country. I didn't see a single hill all the way. There were lots of dairy farms and the houses seemed very different to English houses. They were very quaint and picturesque like cottages on postcards.

When we reached Leuven, we took a taxi to the apartment block where Alicia lived. I was very tired and I slept for the rest of the morning. I woke up hungry so Jack took Rudi and me to a café and that was where I had my tomate aux crevettes and then Dames Blanche in the ice cream parlour, with Spa water to drink.

Rudi was eager to introduce me to his friends from the block so Jack left us to walk back and he went to Alicia and Paul's shop in the centre of town. They had a news agent's kiosk. There were three large rectangular blocks of apartments forming three sides of a square and in the centre of the square was a hexagonal shaped tower block. All the blocks had grass surrounds, and behind the far block was a playground area with climbing frames and picnic tables. It was here that all the kids congregated. Rudi had been telling them for some weeks that an English girl was coming to stay with him, and they were all waiting to see his foreign visitor. I felt like a celebrity as they watched us approach across the grass.

I met Chantelle, a small pretty girl with blond ringlets and beautiful white teeth when she smiled. Then I was introduced to Paula and Ingrid who were twins with long dark hair and brown eyes. Rudi said that they were actually Dutch girls. There were more boys than girls in the group. There was: Josh with a bad front tooth, Rene, tall with freckles, Bennie, a stout, smiley boy and Emmanuel who they called Mani. There was also a boy who looked older than the others. They called him Jeff and his mop of hair was so blond that it was white. He was smoking, and when introduced to me, he shrugged and nodded then turned away.

I liked them all except Jeff who never spoke to me but obviously spoke about me in Flemish to the others. He would glance at me and say something which nobody would translate for me and made everyone look as if they felt a little awkward. Chantelle seemed to enjoy it though as she giggled whenever he did this.

Later on Rudi told me that the boy, who they called Jeff the white boy, on account of his white hair, didn't usually hang around with them, and he also said that Chantelle was not as nice as the others. Alicia said that she was very spoilt because her family constantly bragged about how

119

pretty she was, and they let her have anything she wanted. But it was true, she was lovely looking. Rudi was right, and the boy Jeff, didn't join us for some days after this first meeting and I was able to relax and get to know the others, keeping it in mind that I should be wary of Chantelle. Rudi spoke English fluently, but the others had varied abilities ranging from just a few words to being able to form simple phrases. Chantelle was probably the best. Anyhow for all of them, their English surpassed my Flemish which was non-existent.

Rene was my favourite character in the group. I used to sing the Four Tops song, 'Don't Walk Away Rene' and he loved it. I also liked Bennie the smiley boy and I would say, "Not many Bennie," which was a phrase my school friends used when they wanted to affirm something. He liked me saying it and all the others started to copy and say it, which made him laugh.

I got to know other people who were not particular friends of Rudi. Alicia's neighbour and friend had two daughters. The older of the girls Janette, was my age. The mother Anna, was a beautiful woman who reminded me of Elizabeth Taylor with her very dark hair and large dark eyes. Her husband had Clark Gable type looks, moustache notwithstanding. Janette became my friend. She had long blond hair and blue eyes, but Freda her younger sister was dark haired like her parents.

I told Alicia that I liked Janette and her family, and she began to tell me a little about them. She said that Anna had been her friend for many years, having been neighbours through their teenage years. Anna had met a boy named Pierre when she was eighteen and they were together for a couple of years. Pierre's parents didn't approve of Anna because they were quite wealthy, and she was an ordinary girl who worked in a shop. He was put under pressure to finish with her and he eventually caved in an ended the relationship. But by then Anna was pregnant. When he told his parents, they threatened him with being cut off from the family, and that meant the money, if he ever had anything to do with her again. Her parents contacted them and they denied that the child was his.

When Janette was born, she had fair hair and Pierre's eyes and complexion. Still his family would have nothing to do with them. Janette was a keen swimmer, and often went to the local pool. She told her mother about a blond man who was sometimes at the pool and was very kind to her, giving her swimming tips. The man was of course Pierre.

Alicia said that when Anna married Fredrik, he had promised to treat Janette as his own child and he seemed to go along with his promise until Freda was born, and since then he had treated Janette unfairly, so Alicia had very little time for Fredrik. I admitted that I found him a little grumpy.

I did not tell Janette that I knew this story of course, but a few days later, I called at Janette's apartment and her father appeared to be in a very bad mood. As we stepped outside, and she closed the door, she seemed very upset, in fact close to tears.

"My father doesn't like me," she said, "It's because I am not a child from him."

I felt very sorry for her and now understood what Alicia meant when she said that he did not treat her fairly.

One day Alicia took me to her Cousin Vera's house. It was a short walk from the apartments, in a long street of terraced houses. Bennie lived in this street as well and so did Alicia's mother. Vera was a short plump woman with silver hair. We sat in her parlour. She didn't speak English, but Alicia translated for her. She was trying to say that her daughter Valerie was out doing some errands but would be delighted to meet me and she would be back soon. Then Vera got out the Genevieve and poured us a small glass each. It was fizzy, it smelt of lemons and something else that I couldn't identify. It tasted a little bitter I thought but I was very polite and said that I liked it. I had no idea that I had, in fact, been drinking gin! Alicia told me later and said that a little wouldn't harm me!

Valerie was a strange girl, she was tiny; older than me but smaller. Her face looked too old for her body. Her complexion was quite dark, as if suntanned and she had very black hair which was backcombed and curled outwards at the ends. It reminded me of my mother's hairstyle, almost 1940's. It also felt stiff to touch, because she wore so much hair lacquer. She took me to the shops, to see the sites of Leuven, and we stopped off at cafes and ice cream parlours. Every time we ran out of things to do she would say, "What now Elleen!" As if I had any idea what we could do!

One day, her uncle joined us. He was eighteen, and blond like Valerie's mother, his sister. His name was Jean, and he took us for a soda drink in the most exciting café I had ever seen. It was down a narrow dead end street and at the bottom of a steep flight of stairs. It was underground, and that was fun in itself, but the walls were white and uneven and covered with strange artefacts ranging: from animal skins, skulls, bones, to torture instruments, chains and traps. The music was loud but very up to date. Jean ordered beer and we had lemon soda. He taught me to count to twenty in Flemish, and he asked me how I liked Belgium.

I loved it, everything about it, from the pretty quaint little houses to the hustle and bustle of this busy little university town, home to a brewery where a famous Belgian beer is made. I loved the stunning medieval architecture, and the Al Fresco dining. Belgian chips and Belgian ice cream were the best in the world. The quirky café with its macabre décor became a favourite haunt of mine in all my subsequent visits to Leuven.

The journey back to London came all too quickly. I was happy to be travelling with Alicia, but sad to have left Rudi and his gang of friends, lovely kind Janette, and of course crazy Valerie with her constant what now Elleen, and her sparse knowledge of English which was better than my Flemish!

The following year I was back! Same arrangements, I

travelled across with Jack, but this time I was going to be staying for a month. I emerged after my morning sleep on arrival, having travelled all night, and the whole gang were waiting for me, on the wall outside the block. I saw myself as a bit of a celebrity and thought it would be clever to pretend that I didn't notice them. I walked past them and turned the corner towards the shops. I bought some post cards then returned. This time Rudi had come down so I had to stop. I wanted to really but thought that they would regard me as the mysterious foreign girl if I acted slightly aloof. I even thought it had worked and made them more eager to see me. They were all there; Chantelle, Bennie, Ingrid and Paula, Mani, Josh and Renee. Bennie was to have a birthday party later in the week, and I was invited.

The next day, Rudi had an appointment at the asthma clinic, and I went to Janette's. We decided to go out, but when we got downstairs, the gang were all there again, but to my horror the odious blond boy Jeff was with them. He was still smirking and obviously talking about me not to me. Chantelle had started her giggling again at his sly comments, but the rest of them asked us to join them as they were going to walk to the small river. I didn't know where it was but I followed and Janette seemed quite happy to come along.

We walked along the street where Bennie lived and Valerie, and then through another two streets and under a bridge. We then came to a grassy bank by a small stream. It was not much of a river. The grass was dry and scrub like, it wasn't even pretty there. This had been a waste of time. In a beautiful town like Leuven, we had come to an ugly barren place. We walked along and eventually reached some benches where we all sat down. Then the boy Jeff got out cigarettes and started handing them out. Now I understood, they had come here to smoke!!

It was remote and they couldn't be seen. Not that Jeff was worried about that, he smoked anywhere. They were paying him thirty Belgian Francs for a cigarette. He offered one to me and I declined, so did Janette. Then he started smirking again and made a comment. I picked up the word Kinder, which I thought meant children.

We walked back slowly and I was relieved to get away from that horrible Jeff. What made things even worse was that Rudi and Alicia were back and she was very cross because I had wandered off and she didn't know where I had gone. I blamed Jeff and hoped that I wouldn't see him again. However Jeff was to cause me more trouble!

A few days later the gang were gathered outside the apartments and Janette and I went downstairs. Jeff wasn't there so we joined them. Rudi was still upstairs as he had just taken medication and had to wait for it to take effect. We sat on the wall outside, and were there for a few minutes when an elderly man came out of the apartment lobby and began ranting and gesticulating angrily. I had no idea who he was or what it was about, but realised that they were all looking at me. As he walked away, he looked at me and tossed his head as though he was disgusted. I thought that perhaps he didn't like English people!

Chantelle was giggling and ecstatic and she said in her best English, "Oooh what have you been doing with Jeff, the white boy, last night?" I looked at her slightly puzzled, but mainly horrified and asked, "What do you mean? I was in Alicia's all night, I didn't go anywhere last night!"

"Well the man, Mijnheer Vaas saw you kissing and touching with the white boy last night!"

"Oh no he did not!" I exclaimed.

"But he saw you," and by this time I was getting angry. I hated that Jeff and I wouldn't have gone anywhere near him.

Alicia was at the shop working whilst Paul had his lunch break and Rudi was with her helping. So I asked Janette if we could go and get her mother to help. Janette told her exactly what had been said and the three of us marched down to the ground floor to confront Mijnheer Vaas. He began ranting in Flemish again and pointing at me. I shook my head and said, "It wasn't me. It was obviously someone else!" Anna translated to him in case there was any doubt that he understood. Then she told me that he still insisted that it was me and he saw me. Anna said that he was refusing to back down or be reasonable.

When Alicia returned, Anna told her about the whole business. Alicia was slightly amused but she could see how upset I was and said that she was going to sort it out and put an end to it. So she went to tackle Mijnheer Vaas, and when she reappeared ten minutes later, she said a Flemish swearword, which I knew because Rudi had told me it. Then she continued, "Stupid, miserable old fool. I told him that you were in here all night and he still insisted that he saw you with the boy. Who is the boy anyway?"

Rudi explained that he was someone Josh and Mani knew, and that he wasn't very nice. Alicia was furious because Mijnheer Vaas had as good as called her a liar. Alicia had dared him never to come near me or Rudi again. I never found out why he said those things about me, but thought that he really didn't like foreign people.

When Alicia had calmed down she said that we should all forget about it and she had my favourite lunch which was Mett mit brood. This was raw minced pork spread on bread with mustard. My other favourite was toast Cannibal which was raw beef on toast. Whenever I order these things in restaurants, they always say that I can't be English if I eat this!

Rudi told the others that none of Mijnheer Vaas's accusations were true, and the only one to carry on talking about it was Chantelle until Rudi lost his temper and shouted at her.

The holiday, in spite of this incident, was really fantastic. Paul was able to get a stand in to mind the shop so he could take some holiday. We went to France, Luxemburg, Holland and Germany. Rudi and I had fun singing in the car and playing games to pass the time on our journeys. Our favourite thing was to sing duets such as, 'Cinderella Rockefeller', and I would be Abi and he would be Esther and put on a high voice. I was proud to have been to so many countries and couldn't wait to tell my friends in England.

A cinema in Bruxelles was showing a re-run of 'Gone with the Wind', which was Alicia's favourite film. So we all went to see it. I thought it was the best film I had ever seen and that Vivien Leigh was the most beautiful woman I had seen.

Rudi and I went to the party at Bennie's house. I said that if white Jeff was there I was coming straight back. But he wasn't. There was lots of dancing, to mostly English pop music, and in the middle of the party there was a violent thunder storm, which really added atmosphere to the darkened room. I now think of it as being like a scene from the Rocky Horror show. It was great fun.

The party finished at nine o'clock, and as most of us were walking back to the apartments, no adults had to collect us.

The following year I came completely by myself with no Jack to escort me, and the year after that, Lizzy came with me. By that time Alicia and Paul had sold the apartment and bought a large house outside Leuven, where she could have her parents living with them in their old age. This was the year they took us to Bruges, where I have friends now, who I visit often. After Alicia's parents died, and Rudi married, the family moved to the USA.

The Love of Books

Proust said, 'There are perhaps no days of our childhood we lived so fully as those we spent with a favourite book'.

My love of reading began at a very early age. At five I quickly outgrew Janet and John books and progressed to something more substantial like Topsy and Tim, and Lucy Atwell. But I finished all of those and wanted more. So I read Milly Molly Mandy stories and My Naughty Little Sister. But one day I read something which transported me to a fantasy world and it was a revelation that a simple book could feed the imagination so easily. Reading, 'The Water Babies', took me to a world where people don't die, they live in a different place. I knew nothing about Kingsley's religious parodies, just that I might not have to die like Mrs Rust died, or maybe she didn't!

I read some of the books from Lizzy's bookcase. Many of them were ballet novels about girls who dreamed of becoming prima ballerinas and then did. So then I wanted to be a ballerina and I joined a local dancing school to learn Ballet and tap dancing, but I hated it!

Then I read the Katie novels by Susan Coolidge, and the Little Women series. I found it very easy to become the characters and imagine doing the things they did. In Little Women, I was Amy because she was nearest to my age and I loved the part where they went ice skating and Amy fell through the ice and had to be rescued. Then she made up with Jo who had been angry with her for burning her book. I imagined Lizzy making a big fuss of me like Jo did Amy so relieved that she was alright after the ordeal.

One day Sharon told me about a book she had borrowed from the library. She said that in the story some children go through a wardrobe and come out into another world where there is a witch and a lion. So I joined the library and the first book I borrowed was, 'The Lion, the Witch and the Wardrobe'. I saw myself as Susan because I thought that Lucy was a bit too self-righteous for me. I imagined Susan as a pretty girl with long fair hair, a bit like Sharon. That was how I wanted to be. I was immersed in the story and had a guilty admiration for Jadis, the white witch. I later read the other books in the Narnia series, but none of them had quite the effect on me as the first one I read.

When I was ten, I discovered something else about books. Not all books were stories. I knew we had maths and English books in school, but I wouldn't have taken those home to read. But in the library, I came across Patrick Moore's guide to astronomy. I was looking for a third book to fill my ticket allowance, and so I borrowed it. From then on I developed a great new interest. I knew that there was the sun and moon and Mars, but I had never heard of the Solar System. I did not know that there was Jupiter, or Saturn with rings, or a Stellar System with constellations, nebulas and galaxies.

These were the most fascinating facts I had ever learnt about and I then borrowed book after book on the subject until I had gone through the entire collection in the junior library. I was quite an expert by this time and I studied star maps and on clear nights, I could find all the constellations visible at that time of the year.

For my eleventh birthday my parents bought me a huge astronomy encyclopaedia, and then a telescope for Christmas. I didn't care how cold it was outside, I was in the garden with my four inch reflector, night after night. I saw the moons of Jupiter, the rings of Saturn and the Horses Head Nebula in Orion. I told my cousin Sue about the Solar System and she said that lots of stars probably had Solar Systems of their own. This was probably the first time we had a serious discussion and our parents thought it was hilarious listening to us contemplating the possibility of extra-terrestrial life.

Then I wrote my own Illustrated Guide to Astronomy and I won a prize at school for it.

I won two more prizes that year. One was for a story I wrote about visiting Ann in Canada. I had never been there but imagined myself travelling, watching a movie and having food and wine on the aeroplane. I was of course much older, or else I wouldn't have had wine.

The other prize I won was for a school project about Winston Churchill after he died. Sharon had moved to Woodford, and on the green near her house, there was a statue of Churchill. So I made a statue of Churchill from papier mache, covered it with plaster of paris, and painted it black like the one on the green. I won a book about Prince Andrew when he was a little boy playing with the corgis.

My love of reading prompted me to study Literature and I submitted a selection of my own poems and stories for my dissertation, which was well received, and gained me a merit.

By reading books, I have been transported into the lives of: Elizabeth Bennett and Lisbeth Salander, Jane Eyre and Jane Marples, Bathsheba Everdene and Katniss Everdeen, Lady Macbeth and Lady Bracknell. This is to name but a few. Jojen said, 'A reader lives a thousand lives before he dies', and George RR Martin added, 'A man who never reads lives only one'.

Acknowledgements

Many thanks to New Generation Publishers for advice and the means to actually make this happen.

To all my friends and family who have jogged my memory about the way things were and what we got up to! And to Rula for letting me hijack her story.

To my wonderful daughter for choosing the right university, providing me with the excuse for many visits to a truly inspirational part of the country, where I could write in peace and tranquillity.

Special thanks to the friendly staff at Loch Fyne and Milsoms Hotel, Kenilworth, where a great part of my writing was done in the relaxed comfortable atmosphere of the snug. It was often accompanied by coffee and more often by Prosecco!

Gratitude to all friends who helped and encouraged me to carry on, even when times were difficult. Thanks to Mo for the advice and literature on book structure and writing.

Finally, thanks to the people of East London for being such colourful and entertaining characters, providing a backdrop for these stories.

Lightning Source UK Ltd.
Milton Keynes UK
UKHW04f0617221018
330961UK00002B/596/P